FAMILY

· *A Celebration* ·

Edited by Margaret Campbell — Photographs by Joan Beard

PETERSON'S

Princeton, New Jersey

EDITORIAL DIRECTION BY CAROL HUPPING   ART DIRECTION BY LINDA HUBER
PRODUCTION SUPERVISION BY BERNADETTE BOYLAN   BOOK DESIGN BY KATHY KIKKERT
PROOFREADING BY MARIE BURNETT   COMPOSITION BY GARY ROZMIERSKI

Library of Congress Cataloging-in-Publication Data

Campbell, Margaret.

    Family : a celebration / Margaret Campbell.

        p.   cm.

    ISBN 1-56079-468-2

    1. Family. I. Title.

HQ503.C35   1995

306.85—dc20   9534486

                                                                        CIP

Printed in the United States of America

10 9 8 7 6 5 4 3 2

Visit Peterson's on the Internet (World Wide Web) at

http://www.petersons.com

(continued on page 179)

To my mother Claire Campbell (1919-1984),

who would have loved this book,

and to my daughter Claire, who already does.

—M.C.

To my mother,

who is as excited about this book as I am,

to the individuals who helped me find families,

and to those families who let me take their pictures.

—J.B.

CONTENTS

Introduction · *Margaret Campbell* · viii

ACKNOWLEDGMENTS

To all the poets and writers included in this book, I send my special thanks for the vitality of their art and the joy it brings to readers like myself. I am particularly grateful to Al Maginnes, Pete Fromm, Bobbie Su Nadal, Roger Weingarten, and Ellen Lesser who, early in this project, by returning my phone calls and answering my letters with enthusiasm and respect, helped me to understand the importance of this book. A special thanks must also go to the literary agents and publishing people who heard my pleas for prompt turn-around on permission agreements and responded favorably. And to over 350 writers around the country who submitted work, I'd like to say that your warm letters of support made me feel part of a large literary family.

I am personally grateful to Linda Voorsanger, Yvonne Mattos, Barbara Stern, Alice Krause, Sally Cowan, Linda Meyer, Elijah Cobb, Gilda Latzky, my cousin Amanda Smith, and many others who suggested writers for this book and who took a personal interest in the project. And thanks to Edyta Zielinska and Darlan Harris for helping me with my correspondence.

I would not have known what this book is all about if it weren't for a circle of women friends from whom I have learned so much about the meaning of love: Carol Grener, Nancy Bailey, Brenda Bortz, and my editor, Carol Hupping, who should be credited with the original idea that led to this book and for her gentle but firm and familial approach to bringing out the best in me.

I would also like to thank Linda Huber, Peterson's art director, who worked tirelessly to make this book a work of visual beauty, and Joan Beard, whose photographs capture the essence of this book. I am also grateful to Joan Beard for the chance to share this unique experience with a kindred spirit. And to all the staff at Peterson's, a heartfelt thanks.

My deepest thanks is extended to my husband, Curt Rowell, whose encouragement and support were unflagging, and my daughter, Claire, who made sure that I never lost touch with the ebb and flow of family life.

—M.C.

INTRODUCTION

My most positive childhood memories of family life played themselves out on the stage of the small but busy West Philadelphia row house of my Aunt Mildred and Uncle Bev. There, I found my extended family of quirky aunts, uncles, and cousins—an entertaining relief from the isolated life my mother, father, and I knew. Everything about 1947 Redfield Street encouraged the gathering of family, friends, and neighbors, from the front porch with the green metal chairs and the green striped awning to the postage stamp backyard where there was enough room to relax and play while the laundry dried. Behind the house was a vast orphanage at which I would often gaze from the upstairs rear window, wondering who the children were who lived there and what would become of them once they left. What I

never seemed to realize was that Aunt Mildred's was an orphanage, too, a place where family members in need or crisis were always welcome. My grandmother You-You lived there. Uncle Leslie lived there. Cousin Jack and Cousin Carol were raised there. I even spent one summer there while my mother worked at a pharmaceutical plant nearby. Mildred's husband and daughter, both named Beverly, somehow accepted their mother's desire to share their home with so many relatives, but I don't think it was always easy. And Aunt Mildred's generosity was delivered with a strict sense of propriety, order, and family loyalty. She was not always sweet and sympathetic, but she was responsible.

In Aunt Mildred's house, all first names were preceded by the empowering possessive adjective: Our.

Leslie was not just Leslie; he was Our Leslie. Jack was not just Jack; he was Our Jack. Teenie was not just Teenie; she was Our Teenie. For me there was something magical about the our-word. Whenever I heard it, I felt the warm, enveloping glow of the family—the sense that I belonged to something larger and more enduring than my own little self.

There I grew to love the movement of families: the family choreography, as my theatrical Uncle Leslie called it. Someone was always going somewhere, leaving the room, entering the room, going to the bathroom, going to the store, making announcements (We're expecting Uncle Drew and his tribe in half an hour") or pronouncements ("There will be no more jumping on the sofa, is that clear?"). Someone was always reading a book or magazine, spreading the newspaper out on the dining room table, tinkering with some toy or gadget, or staring out the window waiting for a lover to beep the horn. And everyone was always ready to laugh. The reckless and medicinal laughter I associate with my mother's family transformed the drama of family life in the tiny Philadelphia row house into a domestic American opera.

The idea of the family as an introductory course in the theatre of humanity may be a familiar metaphor to many, but a class project at my daughter's Greenwich Village elementary school earlier this year opened my eyes to the new metaphors for family that our children are forming. The assignment was to produce a family tree, and indeed many children organized their families into treelike structures. But one child envisioned a rainbow, another a merry-go-round, another a circus tent.

Looking up at the colorful display that spanned an entire wall at P.S. 3, I tried to think of other metaphors for family: the prism of family through which life is refracted into a rainbow of relationships and experiences; the web of family that threatens to trap and isolate its members; the bosom of the family that protects and nurtures. My own metaphor for the family is a constellation of planets consisting of a mix of biological and nonbiological family relationships. The closest planet in my family constellation is a circle of women friends whom I have known for more than twenty years and with whom I spend most holidays. Other planets near and far include my husband's family, what remains of my mother's and father's families, the Danish couple who have known me since I was five years old, the Polish family who named me their daughter's godmother, an old boyfriend's family who, during my delicate adolescence taught me how to enjoy life, my former husband's family who always remembers me at Christmas, and our apartment building neighbors, who are now our most immediate and accessible family. I visit my many families as often as I can, in any way I can.

When I look through the writings in this book, I feel my family planetary system expand even further to include dozens of families, real and imaginary, whose intimate moments are revealed in the poems, essays, and stories included here. Much of the writing is "full of family feeling," an expression Maxine Kumin uses to describe her uncles in "The Deaths of the Uncles." In one poem, two sisters decide to become neighbors after forty-five years apart. In another, a father watches his two children strap themselves into his ex-wife's car and thinks about the meaning of divorce. In one essay, a mother reflects on what it means to be an only child. In another, a father thinks about the benefits of growing up in a family that speaks several languages. What all the selections have in common is a belief in the human capacity to form and sustain lasting familial relationships despite hardship and adversity.

As familiar as I am with every selection in this book, I never seem to tire of reading certain pieces over and over again, lingering over the lines that hold special meaning for me. The opening and closing lines of Pattiann Rogers's poem, "The Family Is All There Is," speaks to an idea that has always been the centerpiece of this project for me: the interrelatedness of all life. "Think

of those old, enduring connections found in all flesh. . . . The family—weavers, reachers, winders, and connivers, pumpers, runners, air and bubble riders, rock-sitters, wave-gliders, wire-wobblers, soothers, flagellators—all brothers, sisters, all there is. Name something else."

—M.C.

•　　　•　　　•

As a photographer, I reach out to people with my camera. I try to glean their stories and reveal them in images. Each shot in this book is a fragment of a family's story, a sixtieth of a second, captured from their life, one which I hope will bring to light something essential about them.

When I began this project, friends and relatives asked: What kind of families are you interested in? They frequently assumed I wanted beautiful people, golden children, young married parents with wise, white-haired grandparents enjoying their sunset years. I told them I wasn't looking for superficial beauty but rather the inner beauty that revealed the love and respect families can have for one another. Some people then said they didn't know families like that. In the end, I found many of them.

I found single-parent, two-parent, and sprawling extended families defined by blood and nonblood relations. I saw children who went to whoever was closest when they needed something and who surprised their parents when they spoke easily about their connections. Each family had a unique way of communicating with one another—spoken, unspoken, manifested in looks, gestures, and habits, things that are passed down from parent to child, perhaps for generations, reinvented time and again. I saw the politics of the heart playing itself out in little and big ways. Two parents watching lovingly as their daughter poses for the camera in fifties attire. A dying mother flanked by her offspring. Two cousins inviting me into their private world.

Amidst all the talk of family values by the media and politicians, I found something far more complex and precious. I did not see one type of family that stood out above the rest. There was no correlation between income level and the quality of parenting. Rather I saw that each family struggled to negotiate its own way of working together, especially in front of the inquiring camera.

As I traveled throughout the country working on this book, I visited an island cottage off the coast of Maine, housing projects in New Jersey and Florida, an elaborate mansion in Connecticut, and a funky loft in California. We spoke, ate, laughed, and made pictures. All the families shared their homes, their food, and, most importantly, themselves.

Throughout this project, I asked myself, "Who am I?" There were obvious answers: a single woman without children living in an urban setting, a sister, a daughter, an aunt, a niece, a cousin, a grandchild. As I framed, edited, and cropped my work, I found my definition of family expanded. Distant relations, friends and colleagues, people who nurture me are all part of my broad interpretation of family. Instead of feeling alone in the world, I felt connected and grateful for the opportunity to glimpse into so many lives.

—J.B.

Part 1

·

WHAT A FAMILY IS

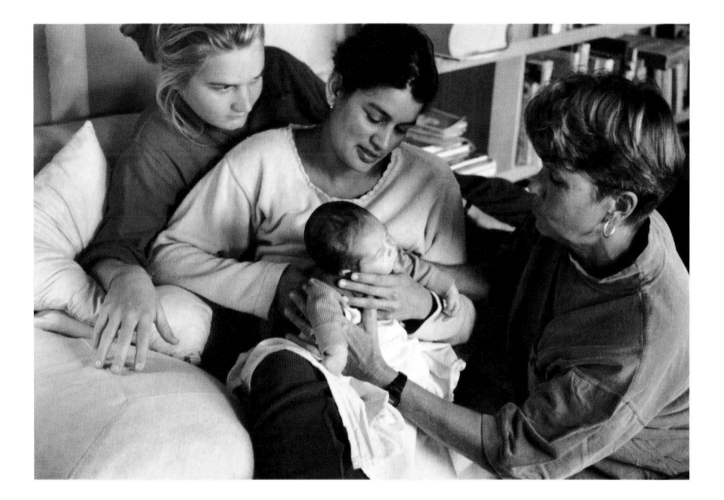

AFRICAN CREATION

Aurora Levins Morales

We begin in Africa, where all stories begin. With the band of a thousand ancestors from whom humanity came. With the one woman out of a thousand we all share as common ancestor. With our abuela. The small, dark woman who is the mother of every woman—every Puerto Rican woman, Chinese woman, English woman, Zulu woman on earth. The one who belongs equally to Harriet Tubman and Eleanor Roosevelt, Guanina and Isabela la Católica, Juana Colón, Lolita Lebrón and Felisa Rincón.

She was never the golden-haired Eve in Renaissance paintings, whose flowing locks fall across perky breasts, munching apples with the snake. She was walnut-skinned with hair like a thundercloud, and her breasts hung long and slack and leathery from nursing many babies. She lived at the rim of the wide and green Sahara, a land of many rivers and flowering meadows, and she did not eat apples. She ate dates from the palms and sweet berries from shrubs. She ate nuts and seeds, wild grubs and honey. She had antelope when she could get it. Fish when she could catch it. She did not live in a garden, alone with a man. She lived with a band of kin, and they walked wherever they pleased, on the green and yellow and brown earth, gathering, and dropping seeds, hunting, and scattering bones, drinking, and going dry, growing older and bearing young, finding and making.

Making people. The children who clung to her body, were strapped on her back, who ran at her calloused heels, who worked at her side, who made new kin and walked away to new gathering grounds. Her children spread outward like a fan of fingers. They followed rivers. They moved along the coasts gathering mussels where river mouths spill fresh water into the sea. They moved south into the grasslands, and farther still, into the green hearts of rainforests. They moved east and west and north around the rim of the Mediterranean and kept spreading, unfurling, filling up continents. They found homes everywhere on earth, and slowly, over hundreds of thousands of years, they changed their bodies to fit the new lands.

Some lived at the edge of the sky, in high cloudy valleys among snowy peaks, and their chests grew broader and deeper in the thin air, their blood richer. Some lived in the dense, dimly lit forests, where warm rain dripped from a canopy full of the swinging shadows of monkeys, and these became quick and light on their feet, small and compact, with smooth and hairless skin, the better to stay cool. Some lived in places of long winter and few plants, of mammoth Arctic nights and blazing days, and they padded themselves with fat against the bone-cracking cold, and learned to eat the oily flesh of whales. Some lived inland, houses pitched against the winds of winter sweeping the plains and steppes for endless months of darkness, far from the fish oils that could strengthen their bones, and these grew pale, translucent skin, made to suck up the meager sunlight. Some stayed in the latitudes of the sun, and gathered up even more of the darkness of earth to keep them from burning. They were tall and thin, arms long enough to pick fruit of savanna trees, legs swift enough to follow the distant herds, with a blue-black sheen that gave their bodies shade.

But everyone in the menagerie came from the same litter, suckled at the same brown breast; and in every one of her daughters, unchanged through the generations, a tiny fragment of her flesh persists, a grain of earth she gave us,* with our humanness, in the wide Saharan garden, at the beginning of human time.

---

* Examining samples of mitochondrial DNA, passed down only from mother to daughters, allowed researchers to come up with the "Eve theory," that although we also have many other ancestors, all human beings have at least one common female ancestor, part of a small band of several thousand humans from whom we evolved, living in sub-Saharan Africa, about 200,000 years ago.

FAMILIES

Jane Howard

Each of us is born into one family not of our choosing. If we're going to go around devising new ones, we might as well have the luxury of picking their members ourselves. Clever picking might result in new families whose benefits would surpass or at least equal those of the old. The new ones by definition cannot spawn us—as soon as they do that, they stop being new—but there is plenty they can do. I have seen them work wonders. As a member in reasonable standing of six or seven tribes in addition to the one I was born to, I have been trying to figure which earmarks are common to both kinds of families.

(1) Good families have a chief, or a heroine, or a founder—someone around whom others cluster, whose achievements as the Yiddish word has it, let them *kvell*, and whose example spurs them on to like feats. Some blood dynasties produce such figures regularly; others languish for as many as five generations between demigods, wondering with each new pregnancy whether this, at last, might be the messianic baby who will redeem us. Look, is there not something gubernatorial about her footstep, or musical about the way he bangs his spoon on his cup? All clans, of all kinds, need such a figure now and then. Sometimes clans based on water rather than blood harbor several such personages at one time. The Bloomsbury Group in London six decades ago was not much hampered by its lack of a temporal history.

(2) Good families have a switchboard operator—someone like my mother who cannot help but keep track of what all the others are up to, who plays Houston

Mission Control to everyone else's Apollo. This role, like the foregoing one, is assumed rather than assigned. Someone always volunteers for it. That person often also has the instincts of an archivist, and feels driven to keep scrapbooks and photograph albums up to date, so that the clan can see proof of its own continuity.

(3) Good families are much to all their members, but everything to none. Good families are fortresses with many windows and doors to the outer world. The blood clans I feel most drawn to were founded by parents who are nearly as devoted to whatever it is they do outside as they are to each other and their children. Their curiosity and passion are contagious. Everybody, where they live, is busy. Paint is spattered on eyeglasses. Mud lurks under fingernails. Person-to-person calls come in the middle of the night from Tokyo and Brussels. Catchers' mitts, ballet slippers, overdue library books and other signs of extrafamilial concerns are everywhere.

(4) Good families are hospitable. Knowing that hosts need guests as much as guests need hosts, they are generous with honorary memberships for friends, whom they urge to come early and often and to stay late. Such clans exude a vivid sense of surrounding rings of relatives, neighbors, teachers, students and godparents, any of whom at any time might break or slide into the inner circle. Inside that circle a wholesome, tacit emotional feudalism develops: you give me protection, I'll give you fealty. Such treaties begin with, but soon go far beyond, the jolly exchange of pie at Thanksgiving for cake on birthdays. It means you can ask me to supervise your children for the fortnight you will be in the hospital, and that however inconvenient this might be for me, I shall manage to. It means I can phone you on what for me is a dreary, wretched Sunday afternoon and for you is the eve of a deadline, knowing you will tell me to come right over, if only to watch you type. It means we need not dissemble. ("To yield to seeming," as Buber wrote, "is man's essential cowardice, to resist it is his essential courage . . . one must at times pay dearly for life lived from the being, but it is never too dear.")

(5) Good families deal squarely with direness. Pity the tribe that doesn't have, and cherish, at least one flamboyant eccentric. Pity too the one that supposes it can avoid for long the woes to which all flesh is heir. Lunacy, bankruptcy, suicide and other unthinkable fates sooner or later afflict the noblest of clans with an undertow of gloom. Family life is a set of givens, someone once told me, and it takes courage to see certain givens as blessings rather than as curses. Contradictions and inconsistencies are givens, too. So is the war against what the Oregon patriarch Kenneth Babbs calls malarkey. "There's always malarkey lurking,

bubbles in the cesspool, fetid bubbles that pop and smell. But I don't put up with malarkey, between my stepkids and my natural ones or anywhere else in the family."

(6) Good families prize their rituals. Nothing welds a family more than these. Rituals are vital especially for clans without histories, because they evoke a past, imply a future, and hint at continuity. No line in the Seder service at Passover reassures more than the last: "Next year in Jerusalem!" A clan becomes more of a clan each time it gathers to observe a fixed ritual (Christmas, birthdays, Thanksgiving, and so on), grieve at a funeral (anyone may come to most funerals; those who do declare their tribalness), and devises a new rite of its own. Equinox breakfasts and all-white dinners can be at least as welding as Memorial Day parades. Several of us in the old *Life* magazine years used to meet for lunch every Pearl Harbor Day, preferably to eat some politically neutral fare like smorgasbord, to "forgive" our only ancestrally Japanese colleague Irene Kubota Neves. For that and other reasons we became, and remain, a sort of family.

"Rituals," a California friend of mine said, "aren't just externals and holidays. They are the performances of our lives. They are a kind of shorthand. They can't be decreed. My mother used to try to decree them. She'd make such a god-damn fuss over what we talked about at dinner, aiming at Topics of Common Interest, topics that celebrated our cohesion as a family. These performances were always hollow, because the phenomenology of the moment got sacrificed for the *idea* of the moment. Real rituals are discovered in retrospect. They emerge around constitutive moments, moments that only happen once, around whose memory meanings cluster. You don't choose those moments. They choose themselves." A lucky clan includes a born mythologizer, like my blood sister, who has the gift of apprehending such a moment when she sees it, and who cannot help but invent new rituals everywhere she goes.

(7) Good families are affectionate. This is of course a matter of style. I know clans whose members greet each other with gingerly handshakes or, in what pass for kisses, with hurried brushes of side jawbones, as if the object were to touch not the lips but the ear. I don't see how such people manage. "The tribe that does not hug," as someone who has been part of many *ad hoc* families recently wrote to me, "is no tribe at all. More and more I realize that everybody, regardless of age, needs to be hugged and comforted in a brotherly or sisterly way now and then. Preferably now."

(8) Good families have a sense of place, which these days is not achieved easily. As Susanne Langer wrote in 1957, "Most people have no home that is a symbol of

their childhood, not even a definite memory of one place to serve that purpose . . . all the old symbols are gone." Once I asked a roomful of supper guests who, if anyone, felt any strong pull to any certain spot on the face of the earth. Everyone was silent, except for a visitor from Bavaria. The rest of us seemed to know all too well what Walker Percy means in *The Moviegoer* when he tells of the "genie-soul of the place which every place has or else is not a place [and which] wherever you go, you must meet and master or else be met and mastered." All that meeting and mastering saps plenty of strength. It also underscores our need for tribal bases of the sort which soaring real estate taxes and splintering families have made all but obsolete.

So what are we to do, those of us whose habit and pleasure and doom is our tendency, as a Georgia lady put it, to "fly off at every other whipstitch?" Think in terms of movable feasts, for a start. Live here, wherever here may be, as if we were going to belong here for the rest of our lives. Learn to hallow whatever ground we happen to stand on or land on. Like medieval knights who took their tapestries along on Crusades, like modern Afghanis with their yurts, we must pack such totems and icons as we can to make short-term quarters feel like home. Pillows, small rugs, watercolors can dispel much of the chilling anonymity of a sublet apartment or motel room.

When we can, we should live in rooms with stoves or fireplaces or anyway candlelight. The ancient saying still is true: Extinguished hearth, extinguished family. Round tables help, too, and as a friend of mine once put it, so do "too many comfortable chairs, with surfaces to put feet on, arranged so as to encourage a maximum of eye contact." Such rooms inspire good talk, of which good clans can never have enough.

(9) Good families, not just the blood kind, find some way to connect with posterity. "To forge a link in the humble chain of being, encircling heirs to ancestors," as Michael Novak has written, "is to walk within a circle of magic as primitive as humans knew in caves." He is talking of course about babies, feeling them leap in wombs, giving them suck. Parenthood, however, is a state which some miss by chance and others by design, and a vocation to which not all are called. Some of us, like the novelist Richard P. Brickner, "look on as others name their children who in turn name their own lives, devising their own flags from their parents' cloth." What are we who lack children to do? Build houses? Plant trees? Write books or symphonies or laws? Perhaps, but even if we do these things, there still should be children on the sidelines, if not at the center, of our lives. It is a sadly impoverished tribe that does not allow access to, and make much of, some children. Not too much, of

course: it has truly been said that never in history have so many educated people devoted so much attention to so few children. Attention, in excess, can turn to fawning, which isn't much better than neglect. Still, if we don't regularly see and talk to and laugh with people who can expect to outlive us by twenty years or so, we had better get busy and find some.

(10) Good families also honor their elders. The wider the age range, the stronger the tribe. Jean-Paul Sartre and Margaret Mead, to name two spectacularly confident former children, have both remarked on the central importance of grandparents in their own early lives. Grandparents now are in much more abundant supply than they were a generation or two ago when old age was more rare. If actual grandparents are not at hand, no family should have too hard a time finding substitute ones to whom to give unfeigned homage. The Soviet Union's enchantment with day care centers, I have heard, stems at least in part from the state's eagerness to keep children away from their presumably subversive grandparents. Let that be a lesson to clans based on interest as well as to those based on genes.

THE FAMILY IS ALL THERE IS

Pattiann Rogers

Think of those old, enduring connections
found in all flesh—the channeling
wires and threads, vacuoles, granules,
plasma and pods, purple veins, ascending
boles and coral sapwood (sugar-
and light-filled), those common ligaments,
filaments, fibers and canals.

Seminal to all kin is the open
mouth—in heart urchin and octopus belly,
in catfish, moonfish, forest lily,
and rugosa rose, in thirsty magpie,
wailing cat cub, barker, yodeler,
yawning coati.

And there is a pervasive clasping
common to the clan—the hard nails
of lichen and ivy sucker
on the church wall, the bean tendril
and the taproot, the bolted coupling
of crane flies, the hold of the shearwater
on its morning squid, guanine

to cytosine, adenine to thymine,
fingers around fingers, the grip
of the voice on presence, the grasp
of the self on place.

Remember the same hair on pygmy
dormouse and yellow-necked caterpillar,
covering red baboon, thistle seed
and willow herb? Remember the similar
snorts of warthog, walrus, male moose
and sumo wrestler? Remember the familiar
whinny and shimmer found in river birches,
bay mares and bullfrog tadpoles,
in children playing at shoulder tag
on a summer lawn?

The family—weavers, reachers, winders,
and connivers, pumpers, runners, air
and bubble riders, rock-sitters, wave-gliders,
wire-wobblers, soothers, flagellators—all
brothers, sisters, all there is.

Name something else.

NIKKI-ROASA

Nikki Giovanni

childhood remembrances are always a drag
if you're Black
you always remember things like living in Woodlawn
with no inside toilet
and if you become famous or something
they never talk about how happy you were to have your mother
all to yourself and
how good the water felt when you got your bath from one of those
big tubs that folk in chicago barbecue in
and somehow when you talk about home
it never gets across how much you
understand their feelings
as the whole family attended meetings about Hollydale
and even though you remember

your biographers never understand
your father's pain as he sells his stock
and another dream goes
and though you're poor it isn't poverty that
concerns you
and though they fought a lot
it isn't your father's drinking that makes any difference
but only that everybody is together and you
and your sister have happy birthdays and very good christ-
masses and I really hope no white person ever has cause to
write about me because they never understand Black love
is Black wealth and they'll probably talk about my hard
childhood and never understand that all the while I was
quite happy

RELATIVE TRADE

Mariann Ritzer

This is trade day, giveaway day
and I'll take Jennifer Kruger's grandmother
who smells like fresh-baked oatmeal bread
and trade my gnarly, wrinkled, liver-spotted,
cabbage-smelling grandma with the babushkas
she ties tightly under her chin and mine.
I'll grab Henry Kowalski's father with his
sweat shirts and swear words and his slow
pitches in the backyard and give Henry
my stoic, gray-eyed, Bible-quoting father.
I'll trade Martha Bittle's red-lipped, light blonde
mother with painted nails, quick laughter and arms
put there for hugging and give Martha my frail,
driven-by-migraine-headaches mother who dusts
the window sills thrice weekly and eats bran muffins
with raisins on Mondays and Fridays.
I'll take Millie Roiden's Aunt Sassy,
who reads romance novels and whispers
the love scenes to us in a husky, steamy voice

and wears three-inch heels and cracks Juicy Fruit gum
between her beautiful, straight, white teeth.
Yes, I'll take her and give Millie
my Aunt Betsy and her five black cats
with green, glow-in-the-dark eyes who walk
and stalk her efficiency apartment
like burglars in the night.
If they won't agree to an outright trade
I'll play marbles and throw my
winnings in for their people. I'll trade
even-Steven and they'll thank me grandly
for giving them my people and the marbles
and this will be one time they won't call
me an Indian giver. This time I'll play
for keeps and surprise the hell out of them
and when I am rich and famous because of all
the genes I acquired through that thing called
osmosis I'll thank them publicly for playing
the game according to Hoyle and give them each

a crisp, snappy, new dollar bill
and tell them not to spend it all
in one place, like my grandpa says.
I'll keep track of my people, once in a while,
like every month or so, just to see
how things are going, but I won't want them back

nor will I miss them or the bran muffins
with the raisins, the tightly tied babushka,
the black, green-eyed apartment
or the preaching Bible verses
Praise Be The Lord, Amen.

ADOPTING GRIEF

Sandi Sonnenfeld

In 1970, when I was seven years old, my family inherited three cousins, Andy, Leslie, and Julie, who had been left to us by my aunt and uncle's will. At least, that is how my father explained it to my brother, my two sisters and me—that we had been given a special and final gift—the gift of family.

We were close to these cousins—Aunt Jeanie was my father's only sibling, and the two families lived in neighboring towns, a mere fifteen-minute drive between their home and ours. Before Aunt Jeanie died of leukemia, we spent nearly every Sunday at their house—especially in the summer. Aunt Jeanie and Uncle Gerry had a pool—we didn't.

I had always envied my cousins. I envied them because they were all older than I, because Leslie and Julie were twins, which seemed to guarantee a permanent playmate, and because I found my aunt more beautiful than my own mother, perhaps because Aunt Jeanie tanned herself lying on an inflated raft in the blue, chlorinated waters of their pool.

My mother hated the heat, talked endlessly about perspiration and sun poisoning, all the while sitting in a lawn chair under a shady elm tree a few feet away from the water. Even so protected, she always wore a floppy, terry cloth hat imprinted with giant red and blue flowers.

I heard my mother once speculate that Aunt Jeanie got leukemia from breathing in the chemicals from the chlorine. That seemed a warning to me somehow—a warning about the danger too much pleasure brings, at the rapid way life could turn to death.

Such a cautionary note seemed reinforced when my uncle died of a heart-attack on the eleventh green of the local golf course, barely a year after burying his wife. Change suddenly frightened me, anything new, anything different had a darker underbelly, a shadowy hint that disaster could strike at any moment.

But I didn't tell anyone how I felt. My father, my handsome, intelligent father, had told us not to dwell too long on sad things.

I always wondered if he told this to Leslie, Julie and Andy as well, for the day they moved into our house felt like a party, with lots of laughter, noisy conversations, and the endless sound of furniture being rearranged.

"We're one big happy family now," my father said that day. "Brothers and sisters love each other, so play nice, help each other out, and get along."

We did become a bigger family, and certainly a more exciting one. But the excitement evolved from chaos, from the painful effort of blending two families into one.

The Brady Bunch aired the same year my cousins came to live with us. I watched the show every week, fascinated at the similarity of the premise. There were six children in the Brady family; there were now seven in ours. Mike Brady, the father, gave similar lectures about getting along that my father gave. Of course, my mother didn't have an Alice, a housekeeper to help with the cooking and cleaning, an oversight that resulted in weekly and highly vocal arguments between my parents. (This being the real world, of course, when my father told my mother to go ahead and hire someone, she pointed out that with seven kids to raise and send to college there was little money for such things.)

But what I didn't realize then was that the Brady kids had each suffered a loss (the girls had lost their father, the boys their mother) before all coming together. In my family, my cousins had lost both a mother and a father—I and my "real" siblings hadn't lost anyone. The sides weren't equal from the beginning.

Still equity became a major theme in our house. Dad, a fairly prominent New York attorney, who had twice argued successfully before the U.S. Supreme Court, believed strongly in a sense of fair play.

"I love all my children equally," my father once said to a neighbor. "All exactly the same." I, who tended to hover near my father as much as possible, was never sure if he said it for my benefit or for the neighbor's. I do know that the statement hurt me, for I adored my father as only an eight-year-old child can, and in my mind *fairness* dictated that he felt the same about me.

Later in my adolescence, I realized that while my father believed it right to love his children equally, he never really did so, tending always to be just a little bit prouder of his "natural" children's accomplishments (Amy's musical ability, Rick's numerous prizes for scholastic achievement, my own desire to write) than my cousins', probably because our abilities and interests were more like his own.

I will never forget my father's angry disappointment when he discovered Andy was growing two or three marijuana plants in his bedroom. It never dawned on him that my brother Rick had helped smuggle in the plants and probably indulged in joints even more often than Andy did.

And none of us kids, including Andy, who bore the brunt of that anger, did anything to dispel his illusions. We wanted our parents, especially our father, to be proud of us.

To the world, we were the model family. My parents nearly became saints at our local synagogue, if Jewish saints were allowed, and I remember hearing murmurings among the congregation as the nine of us filed into the sanctuary, occupying an entire pew.

My choral teacher at school once asked me if I was Catholic, because she had never heard of a Jewish family having so many children. (I was the third family member she had taught in five years.) I did nothing to dissuade her impression that all of us were born of the same parents. I felt it would be too shameful to admit that

grief was our true mother. I felt too ashamed to admit that I resented being part of so large a family and yet for some reason always experienced loneliness. And I felt too ashamed to admit that while I knew it was nobody's fault, I always hated being different from other families.

One of my friends in elementary school, Patty Anderson, who also happened to live right next door to us, threatened to beat me up once because her mother had scolded her daughters for not getting along better like the Sonnenfeld kids did.

"There's only three of you," her mother had said. "And yet you fight and bicker all the time. There are seven of them, and they always play nicely together. I've never seen them fight or raise their voices."

I looked at my friend in disbelief, recalling how only the night before at dinner when the noise level had risen above a comfortable roar, my mother threatened to turn off her hearing aid, a device she wore as a result of a childhood bout with German measles.

"I'm tuning you out," my mother would say. And then we would hear a strange beep and high-pitch static as she fiddled with a tiny switch in her ear. I know that my older brothers and sisters found it funny. In fact, sometimes I think they intentionally raised the pitch of their voices to see how much she could take. Leslie or Rick would deliberately say something shocking, like they had failed all their classes or blown up the chemistry lab, testing to see if my mother really did turn the hearing aid off or just lowered the volume.

As for myself, I simply found it terrifying—that my mother had the ability to turn us, me, off. She had never done it when only four children lived in the house. I worried sometimes that one day she would turn her hearing aid off permanently, and my mother would forever be removed from me—as inaccessible as being dead.

And surely all that dinner table talk must have served as a barrier against despair, a way to keep grief and confusion at bay. Still, it surfaced in odd ways, like Julie's fascination with much-publicized disasters. She always seemed to know just exactly how many people had died in a recent plane crash, or that an earthquake had just occurred in China. Thinking about it now, memorizing such facts must have been a way to establish control, that if she could keep track of all the world's disasters, perhaps she would be able to predict a crisis closer to home. She didn't want to be caught off-guard.

Neither did I, which is why a few years later when my mother scheduled hourly appointments with us once a month to catch up on our individual lives, I remained cautious.

"Talk to me," my mother would say. "Tell me about school. I never have time with all the other children around, but now we're alone. Talk to me. You never tell me anything."

But I would sit on the edge of my parents' giant king-sized bed and shake my head.

"School's fine," I'd say and volunteer little else. I feared telling her anything secret or important, anything "bad," for she might reach up to her ear and turn off her device, severing all connections between us.

Maybe that was why on the day my friend threatened to beat me up, I looked at her in disbelief, but did nothing to correct her misconceptions about us.

I think we were better actors in this game than any of us ever realized. Children of the sitcom age, we somehow wanted the Brady Bunch myth to be true—even though we knew deep down that two families thrown together out of grief and necessity rather than choice—could never really blend, especially when my cousins came to us already half-grown, fully invested with their own values and belief systems. Through most of our childhood, we lived in a world of half-truths and strong secret resentments, perhaps all the more powerful because the resentments festered in silence.

But this tacit agreement to keep silent, to keep my father and most of the rest of the world in ignorance, was perhaps also the greatest unifying factor among us children. For despite ourselves, we did eventually find a way to exist as a family.

Four years after they moved in, my cousins officially became my brothers and sisters. My parents had finally pressed the courts to make the adoption legal, probably because Andy was nearly eighteen years old and would soon be an adult in his own right.

In one of my parents' family albums, there is a picture of us from that day. It was a chilly November morning, with gray skies that threatened a biting rain. Even so, we all got dressed up: the females in dresses, the males in suits; we were going to the chambers of the family court judge, an official proceeding, and as children of an attorney, we knew to take it seriously.

It felt somewhat like a marriage ceremony.

The judge, a balding, white man in his early fifties, asked my parents if they intended to care for my cousins permanently and as full members of our household.

My parents replied they did.

He asked each one of my cousins individually if they wanted to be part of our family.

"Yes," Andy said.

"Yes," Leslie said.

"Yes," Julie said.

Then he turned to the rest of us, to Rick, Amy, Nancy, and myself and asked us if we accepted my cousins as our new brother and sisters.

We shouted in unison that we did and laughed.

My father later said that the judge didn't have to do that, we children really had no formal say in the proceedings, but he got a kick out of so large a family.

The judge was the one who offered to take the picture, out on the steps of the courthouse.

The snapshot shows us all smiling, huddled together on the concrete steps, but oddly it is a colorless picture, reflecting little of the experiences we endured to make it to that courthouse. Our raincoats were khaki-colored. We all wore dark shoes. And not a single one of us had a tan.

INVENTING A FAMILY

Dennis Saleh

You can have daughters, sons.
Parents, if you like. An uncle or an aunt.
All the relations, all in your home.

Point, and your knee is a son,
white, knobby.
He'll follow you. You'll name him.
Just reach down. He's there.
You can hug him. Never be alone.

Across the room imagine a wife.
Stretch her out on the couch.
Put her there, on the couch, like a friend.

Have as many daughters
as you like. Delight in them.
See them as women, grown.
See them as nothing like your knee.
They are your stomach, or your hands.

Have a father, have a mother.
Have anniversaries.
Trouble yourself remembering birthdays,
the seasons moving through your rooms.

Soon you'll never be alone.
Imagine that.
Sitting together. Eating. Talk
in the dark.

Whole rooms full.
Arrange whole nights up.
Everyone talking to everyone.
Father to Mother. Brother to Sister.

Your knees. Your stomach.
Feel so much stirring. Feel yourself.
Never be alone. Never be alone.
Turn over in the dark. Careful.
There's Mother. There's Sister.

NOT FAMILY

Diane Fassel

We are two white women powerful
in business and art, domestic oddities
by every sociologist's calculation.
Sometimes I fear we will never get it together.
There is no word for what we are and without words
I feel lost. I know us in particulars,
like last Christmas eve in the green frame
Hawaiian church. Our brood takes up an entire pew:

your son and his girlfriend, the artist surfer
in one red and one black shoe, the old Sioux Indian,
his wife, their troubled son, his budding dark daughter.
There's no Hawaiian choir like we promised—
just more of the same white Christmas
sucked out arched windows to stars
filmy in damp salt air.

My eyes travel the length of the bench to your eyes
at the other end, all the markers of our relationship
spread between us like the crumbling gravestones
askew in the cemetery outside. We are the nightmare
of the Republican party. Words crack and break
under the weight of us.

Family isn't big enough, *community* too vogue
and *alternative* catches like the curved barb of
a fishhook in the back of the throat. Alternative to what?
A comfort we never sought because it didn't choose us.

I won't cannibalize another language for the word
for us. I'm done taking from others to ease our pain.

Listen, when I'm blue tired with uncertainty
I long for a studio apartment with one
dedicated lover and a quiet cup of tea.
But it's too late for that, the word for
family is erased from my programming.
The cursor is blinking blinking on
a blank screen and the only word
I can come up with for us is: parenthesis.

BUS STOP FAMILY

Barbara Stern

OCTOBER 1: Linda and I are practically strangers, but in the first two weeks of kindergarten our daughters have decided that they're best friends. Now we're at the bus stop putting the girls on the bus for the very first time.

As the bus headlights approach, Jenna and Nikki reach for each other's hands, pulling away impatiently as their nervous mothers try to kiss them goodbye. We watch them climb the steps, still clutching hands and never looking back at us. Finally two little heads appear at a back window. Linda and I throw kisses and wave wildly as the bus turns down Second Avenue. We don't say a word until the taillights disappear.

"We did it!" *"They* did it—*we're* a mess!" "Why are we doing this?" "We must be crazy—they're much too young!"

We must find a way to make this seem okay. We hit on a marvelous strategy: once a week we'll buy a muffin for the bus driver. That way, if there's a terrible accident, he'll rescue our children first. Linda will buy the muffin tomorrow, I'll but one next week.

That settled, Linda rushes to work, and I rush home to call the school. When I hear that the bus arrived safely and the girls are in their classrooms, I look up Linda's number on the class list and manage to say "They're fine" on the answering machine before I burst into tears. "I know you understand why I'm crying," I sob before hanging up the phone.

OCTOBER 8: Now there are three kindergarten moms at the bus stop. When Kimberly discovered that we live near the same bus stop, she decided to overcome her fears and let Lala take the bus.

Today is Lala's first day, and Kimberly is a nervous wreck. Linda and I, of course, are old pros. As we wait at the afternoon bus stop, we recount our first afternoon.

"We ran back and forth on Second Avenue, because we weren't sure where the bus was supposed to stop."

"When it was 5 minutes late, we thought we'd never see our kids again."

"And then when we finally saw it, I was so afraid we'd miss it that I ran right into oncoming traffic!"

Linda and I sound like old veterans re-living a battle. In one short week, we've become war buddies. I knew that Jenna would make new friends in kindergarten, but I didn't expect new friends for myself.

Suddenly the yellow blur of a bus appears. It's time for the daily ritual—stand at the bottom of the steps, reach out for Jenna as she comes flying out of the bus, try to convince her to wear her jacket, and tie her shoelaces. As we leave the bus stop, I'm so engrossed in Jenna's tales of the day that I forget to say goodbye to the bus stop mothers.

October 12: Jenna and I spent 2 hours at the playground after school today. I'm exhausted, and looking forward to a quiet evening after Jenna goes to sleep.

There's a message on my answering machine from Linda. "Call me as soon as you get home. It's important." This doesn't sound good. I puzzle over whether she sounds worried or angry. Maybe Jenna did something terrible to Nikki. Jenna is certainly more aggressive than Nikki, but how bad could it be? Oh well—maybe we're not meant to be friends after all.

I'm nervous as I dial Linda's number, which I've memorized by now. The minute I hear her voice, I know something serious has happened.

"We just got back from the doctor. At first I didn't believe Nikki when she said she had a pebble in her ear. But she kept complaining that it hurt, and sure enough, there was a pebble from the playground. She says that she and Jenna put them in their ears this morning, and Jenna's is still there."

I hear Nikki crying hysterically in the background, and I ask if she's okay. Nikki's fine, but she's worried about Jenna, Linda tells me. She thinks Jenna should go to the doctor right away.

I spend 45 minutes trying to piece together exactly how Nikki (and maybe Jenna) ended up with a pebble in her ear. The more questions I ask, the more outlandish Jenna's explanation becomes. I give up when Jenna vows that the pebbles were flying around the playground and one landed in Nikki's ear. I may never know whether there's a pebble in Jenna's ear.

So much for a quiet evening.

OCTOBER 24: Kimberly met us at the afternoon bus stop with some horrifying news—over the weekend, she was attacked in the hallway of her building. Linda and I are aghast as she tells the details of a man following her, pushing her into the building, and holding his hands around her neck as he demanded her money. We exchange astonished looks as Kimberly describes how she startled him by throwing a pint of Häagen Dazs ice cream in his face.

"My God, you could have been killed!" Linda exclaims.

"What did your neighbors do? Didn't anyone hear you scream?" I imagine people racing out of their apartments, surrounding the attacker, and holding him hostage until the police arrive.

Kimberly calmly informs us that her ground floor neighbor yelled at her for creating such a ruckus. She's an older woman who has been feuding with Kimberly for years. The attacker ran out of the building while Kimberly was trying to convince her neighbor to call the police.

"This is outrageous!" Linda yells. "Have you reported it to the police?"

Just then the bus arrives. We smile our mommy smiles as the kids descend the steps. It's time to give them our undivided attention. "How was your day at school, honey?" we each ask. As usual, the mommies don't even say goodbye to each other as we head home in different directions.

OCTOBER 25: Kimberly, Linda, and I arrive early at the bus stop, as if by unspoken agreement wanting to have as much time as possible to talk about Kimberly's attack. We pick up right where we left off yesterday.

"So, have you called the police yet?" Linda demands.

"I don't know, you guys. I've been thinking about it, and maybe he never meant to hurt me that badly. What if he's just some poor, innocent homeless man? I don't want to hurt him."

"Hurt *him*!" I'm amazed at the vehemence of my response. "He's the one who hurt *you*! What if he's done the same thing to lots of other women? What if he's going to keep doing it? I think you should try to identify him to the police, and press charges so he'll be locked up for awhile!" I ask myself when I developed such a flaming anti-crime attitude, and realize it was after Jenna was born.

OCTOBER 26: Kimberly called the police today. They drove her around the neighborhood, and she spotted her attacker hanging out on a street corner. She had to crouch down in the backseat of the police car while they called a back-up car to arrest him. She'll have to testify against him next week.

NOVEMBER 3: Kimberly is practically in tears when she gets to the bus stop. "The Grand Jury let him go! They actually believed his innocent act! And they treated me like I was just a hysterical woman! Can you believe it?"

For the first time since I've known Kimberly, I hug her. I hold her tight, trying to stop her shaking.

NOVEMBER 10: Jenna has to have ear surgery tomorrow. She *does* have a pebble in her ear. It's probably been there since last month, and by now it's wedged too far down to remove with tweezers.

I can't believe that Jenna will be getting general anesthesia. I try to act nonchalant about it with her, but as soon as she goes to sleep I frantically call friends who are doctors, other friends, my sister, my mother. I'm looking for reassurance and comfort, but I can't seem to get it from anyone.

I wish Linda weren't out of town. I'd feel better if I could talk to her. We'd probably even get a good laugh over the crazy things our daughters have done.

I promised Jenna that we'd call Nikki and tell her the whole story of the surgery when Nikki gets back on Sunday. Jenna fell asleep singing "Nikki and Jenna put pebbles in their ears, pebbles in their ears, pebbles . . . "

NOVEMBER 12: The surgery went really well. Jenna had no bad reaction to the anesthesia. In fact, although the doctor predicted that she'd be sluggish all day, Jenna insisted on going roller-blading 3 hours after we got home. When I wouldn't let her, she did a trampoline show on the bed instead. I was delighted to send her off to school today.

I just got off the phone with Kimberly. She said that she thought about Jenna all day yesterday. It was great to share all the details of the surgery with her. When we realized it was almost time to pick up the kids at the bus stop, I had to ask her last name so I could put her phone number in my book.

NOVEMBER 27: Four days of Thanksgiving weekend, and I've been on the verge of screaming through most of it. Jenna's behavior has been absolutely vile. From the minute she opens her eyes in the morning, she's complaining, whining, and being nasty to me. I swore I'd never guilt-trip her, but it has taken every ounce of self-restraint to keep from screaming *"I'm the one who plays with you, cooks for you, takes you wherever you want to go, and wakes up in the middle of the night to bring you juice when you're thirsty. How dare you speak to me like that!?"* Now I understand the rage my mother felt when she screamed these very same words at me thirty-some-odd years ago.

My mother and sister have been wonderful helping with Jenna, but it seems like it's never enough. I felt so envious today when they went off shopping and to a play. I don't even care so much about shopping or the theater—I just miss the freedom to do what I want, when I want.

Luckily it was warm enough to go to the playground. I want some adult company, preferably someone I can complain to. I see many mothers that I've known for a long time, but I don't want to sit with any of them. Then I spot Kimberly sitting alone, and my spirits soar.

Her tales of her morning match mine. We speculate about whether all 5-year-olds are nasty, and compare names we've been called by our kids.

As if on cue, Lala appears with a scowl on her face. She's angry because Kimberly made her wear a winter jacket and Jenna is wearing a lighter one. "You're a doo-doo face!" she yells at Kimberly. I watch the hurt and rage cross Kimberly's face, and I know how it feels. I touch her shoulder, she turns to me, and unexpectedly we burst out laughing. It's the first time I've felt relaxed all day.

DECEMBER 13: Today Linda and Nikki and Kimberly and Lala came over to bake cookies for the school bake sale. The kids disappear by the 3rd batch of cookies, and by the 5th batch the mommies are planning a simpler recipe for next year's bake sale. We speak easily about the future, assuming without question that our friendship will last.

"We're like the Brady Bunch," quips Linda.

"Yeah, but you and I have to go home to our husbands," Kimberly replies with a trace of bitterness. "Barbara, sometimes I envy you being single."

"You know what keeps me sane being a single parent?" I quickly reply. "Having friends like you."

"And you know what keeps *me* sane being a married parent?" Linda and Kimberly shoot back simultaneously.

We giggle, spontaneously throw our arms around one another, and belt out in our loudest showtune voices, "Having friends like you."

The children come running into the kitchen, gawking at their weird mothers and wondering what we're singing about. Linda tries to explain something about how people who give each other support are like families to one another, but the kids roll their eyes in disbelief. As they return to play in the bedroom, they put their arms around each other and do a perfect imitation of their moms, singing "Having friends like you."

DECEMBER 16: This afternoon the bus doesn't come to the bus stop. By 4 o'clock, all the parents are annoyed, and by 4:15 we're worried sick. When Kimberly calls the school, she's told there's been a slight problem, but the bus will be leaving shortly.

Nikki's dad offers to drive to school to pick up the kids, but there isn't enough space in his car for all the parents and kids. Besides, what if the bus really leaves soon and there's no one waiting when the kids get to the bus stop?

Linda and David decide to drive to the school while Kimberly and I wait at the bus stop. Kimberly and I try to settle in comfortably on the stoop of a building near the bus stop, but it's pouring rain by now and the whole situation is starting to feel ominous.

"Do you think they could have had an accident?" Kimberly finally voices what we're both wondering.

"Oh, I don't think so. I don't think the school would have lied when you called before." As I try to be strong and brave, I think that I sound like Jenna.

I calmly ask Kimberly about her weekend plans, but I know we're both really thinking about spending the night in a hospital emergency room. After awhile we don't even attempt conversation. We glance constantly at our watches. The bus is almost 2 hours late.

Suddenly there is a gaggle of people racing around the corner of 9th Street and Second Avenue. It's Jenna and Nikki and Lala and Linda and David. "It's the bus stop family!" declares Kimberly as we jump up and run toward them. We join together in a wild melee of kids' voices pitched with excitement, adult voices irritated and curious but mostly relieved, and many bodies hugging each other. For a moment, we do feel like one big family.

"What an adventure!" I exclaim. "I bet this'll be a story we all tell our grandchildren someday."

NEIGHBOR FAMILIES

Margaret Campbell

Last night a woman I had just met stood in the doorway of our kitchen describing her living situation in Norwalk, Connecticut: "We moved back to the street where I grew up. My dad lives across the street, and my brother's around the corner. It's great for Amy. She can just run across the street and see her grandfather any time she wants." As she continued with a brief paean to the city of Norwalk, my attention started to drift to fantasies of family compounds. I thought of a man and woman I once visited in Maine whose children built their homes on the family property and raised their children within dinner-bell distance of one another. I thought of my cousin Carol and her husband John who have five of their seven children within driving distance of their home in the San Diego desert. I thought of my friend Nina's sister with her mother-in-law apartment attached to her house inhabited by her husband's mother, who is always ready to baby-sit. I remembered Sue and Doug who left Brooklyn to return to Seattle once the second child arrived so they could be close to their families. It's hard to argue with the comfort and convenience of having family members you like as neighbors. But what do you do when your family is far away and your need for familial support is a daily concern?

You make your neighbors your family, a solution that works best in communities where most of the people are separated from their biological and friendship families. In a big city like New York, we have found that the opportunities to form neighbor families are excellent, despite all the reports of the isolation of city life. Nevertheless, it takes a certain informality in the lifestyle of neighbors for the feeling of family to get started and take hold.

There are three neighbor families on the floor of our apartment building: a grandmother and her grandson down the hall; a father, mother, and two children across the hall; and our family of three. One of the classically neighborly gestures that often brings us together is the simple act of borrowing. One night several months ago, while my daughter and I were reading a few of her favorite Berenstain Bears books, the doorbell rang. It was the boy who lives with his grandmother down the hall. He wanted to borrow a deck of cards to play with his baby-sitter. We have known this boy for many years, and he knows our apartment well enough to walk right in and get the cards. He took his time finding the cards and left at a leisurely pace, promising to return them soon. A few minutes later, the doorbell rang again, and he was back with the cards, wanting to borrow the Monopoly game instead. By the time we had breezed through a few more books, he was back for the chess set, at which point we realized that what we all really wanted was for him to stay for a while. So I let him read the books to my daughter, and I got dinner ready for all of us. Our little community of neighbor families thrives on spontaneity, and the borrowing-returning ritual seems to be a good catalyst for getting us together.

Doing favors for one another also strengthens our neighbor-family bond, but it sometimes takes courage or desperation to ask busy neighbors to do something familial. Earlier this year, in the middle of the day, while my daughter was at school and I was trying to meet some deadline, my neighbor called from a medical center on 34th Street, asking me if I could please bring her son's bunny to the doctor's office as soon as possible. Now, this is the kind of thing families do for one another. Without hesitation, I opened her apartment with the keys I always have on hand, found the bunny, and rushed it up to my neighbor's son. Caught up in her concern for her son's health, I'm sure my neighbor gave no thought to the fact that I was so pleased to be able to do something for them.

Perhaps the most radical example of the neighbor-family lifestyle is the informal merging of two households. Most evenings, the doors to our apartment and the apartment across the hall are wide open with the members of each family moving freely from apartment to apartment gathering up children, borrowing supplies, exchanging news. The children often eat and bathe together, and the mothers and fathers are trusted to parent each other's children with love and respect.

It may seem as if neighbor families require children to develop and thrive, but many single people we know treat their neighbors as family, too. Not too long ago, we visited one of our daughter's baby-sitters, an older woman from Guyana who lives alone on 14th Street. She introduced us to her neighbor, a younger career woman who lives alone in the apartment next door. The two women showed us the garden accessible from the neighbor's apartment where they often eat dinner together. Like an unusually close mother and daughter, the two women laughed comfortably about their unique arrangement, while I wondered just how uncommon it really is.

I remembered the time I lived briefly with a friend who had a spacious apartment at the corner of Sixth Avenue and Bleecker. Next door to her was an older Italian woman who, except for shopping and visiting her son, spent most of her evenings in her apartment. Every night when my friend and I returned home from our jobs, the neighbor's door would open and the coffee hour would begin. Like a grandmother doting over her children, she would sit at the kitchen table and demand a complete accounting of each of our days. "I want to know everything," was her favorite line, and depending on our schedules, which were pretty busy, we told her all we could.

Perhaps the most famous neighbor families are the fictional families preserved in the reruns of "I Love Lucy," "The Honeymooners," and "All in the Family." For many of us, the image of Ethel or Fred Mertz casually entering Lucille Ball and Desi Arnaz's apartment to discuss some wild scheme is a familiar picture of neighbor family trust and intimacy. Likewise, the comic relief of Ed and Trixie Norton's encounters with the Kramdens and the tension between the Jeffersons and the Bunkers have fixed in our psyche the idea that the neighbor relationship is more than borrowing sugar and sharing garden tools.

There are people who make a policy of keeping their distance from the neighbors, abiding by the principle that "good fences make good neighbors," and ensuring that they remain on a polite and respectful plane with the people who live closest to them. There may be some wisdom in that practice, but what one gains in control and predictability, one loses in spontaneity and magic. Neighbor families must be prepared for the unexpected visit, the untimely request, the shift in gears or plans, and the unscheduled social occasions, a tall order for families on a tight schedule. But when the neighbor family works well and the channels of communication are kept open, it creates a feeling of security and harmony that is nurturing to children, supportive of hard-working adults, and comforting to older people who live alone.

Part 2

•

FAMILIES ARE HUMAN

IT HAS ALWAYS BEEN THIS WAY

Luci Tapahonso

For Lori and Willie Edmo

Being born is not the beginning.
Life begins months before the time of birth.

Inside the mother, the baby floats in warm fluid,
and she is careful not to go near noisy or evil places.
She will not cut meat or take part in the killing of food.
Navajo babies were always protected in these ways.

The baby is born and cries out loud,
and the mother murmurs and nurtures the baby.
A pinch of pollen on the baby's tongue
for strong lungs and steady growth.
The belly button dries and falls off.
It is buried near the house so the child
will always return home and help the mother.
It has been this way for centuries among us.

Much care is taken to shape the baby's head well
and to talk and sing to the baby softly in the right way.
It has been this way for centuries among us.

The baby laughs aloud and it is celebrated with rock salt,
lots of food, and relatives laughing.
Everyone passes the baby around.
This is so the child will always be generous,
will always by surrounded by happiness,
and will always be surrounded by lots of relatives.
It has been this way for centuries among us.

The child starts school and leaves with a pinch of pollen
on top of her head and on her tongue.
This is done so the child will think clearly,
listen quietly, and learn well away from home.
The child leaves home with prayers and good thoughts.
It has been this way for centuries among us.

This is how we were raised.
We were raised with care and attention
because it has always been this way.
It has worked well for centuries.

You are here.
Your parents are here.
Your relatives are here.
We are all here together.

It is all this: the care, the prayers, songs,
and our own lives as Navajos we carry with us all the time.
It has been this way for centuries among us.
It has been this way for centuries among us.

WHEN THE CALL CAME

Norbert Krapf

When the call came
I was about to cut the grass
for the first time. Wild
onion and dandelion were
sprouting across the lawn.
Sheaths of lily of the valley
bearing round green bells
were surrounding the lilac.

When the call came
the yellow marsh marigolds
were rising like the sun
against a boulder in
the flower bed. Bees
buzzed around bunches
of purple grape hyacinth.
The operator said, *I have
a collect call from Colombia.
Do you accept the charges?*
I replied, *Yes, I accept.*

When the call came
the leathery leaves
of bloodroot along the ledge
of the stone wall were
wrapped around the stalks
like green sheets on which
white petals lay. Beside
the fishpond the fronds
of maidenhair fern were
unfurling in the sun.
A voice with a Spanish
accent spoke in my ear,
*This is a social worker. We
have a baby girl born eight
days ago. Will you accept her?*

When the call came
the white blossoms
of the wild cherry at the edge

of the woods were fluttering
on black boughs. The tips
of Japanese irises were
pushing through the soil.
Specks of Bibb lettuce

lay like green confetti
on the upper level of
the rock garden. *Yes, we
accept her,* I said. *Yes.*

THE ONLY CHILD

Sue Ellen Thompson

As I was wheeled out of the delivery room in 1980 and lifted delicately onto my hospital bed, I looked at my husband and said, "I'll never go through *that* again." At the time I felt wonderful: The worst physical pain I had ever endured was behind me, I had a perfectly formed seven-pound daughter, I was ravenously hungry, and breakfast was squeaking its way down the hall.

The real ordeal—months of sleep deprivation, the overwhelming responsibility of caring for a helpless infant—still lay ahead of me, but I did not know that during those blissful three days of rest and pampering. I had a baby there to touch and admire when I wanted to. I had a steady stream of visitors bearing gifts. And I had just dropped 17 pounds in 24 hours. The photographs my husband took of me in the hospital bear all of this

out: There I am, pulling my nightgown down tightly over my still-swollen stomach, no make-up, face blotchy with broken blood vessels but with a smile as triumphant as any cover girl's. I'd done it: I'd had a baby.

The Fourth of July, 1984. We arrive at my parents' house in Canterbury, New Hampshire, with our four-year-old daughter, having just returned from a disastrous visit with friends vacationing on Cape Cod. Ten of us—six adults and four small children—crammed into a two-bedroom bungalow. Although our daughter, Thomasin, has never been particularly difficult, we are caught off guard by her willfulness that weekend. Perhaps she is inspired by the presence of so many other children. Perhaps it is the heat. In any case, she is a terror—fussing impatiently over her meal and at one point hurling her half-eaten hamburger across the table at her father, causing a shocked silence to descend on children and adults alike.

By the time we reach Canterbury, I have a raging headache. I immediately sit down at the kitchen table to unburden myself, exaggerating her behavior a little to persuade my parents that their granddaughter is capable of such horrors. "Well, I hate to say it," my mother comments after listening to my tale of parental woe, "but it's probably because she's an only child." I am too stunned by her rebuke to respond.

Later that evening the assembled family members—my parents, my two sisters and two brothers and their assorted mates and offspring—crowd into the two largest station wagons to go to the fireworks in Concord, the state capital. It is a moonless night, and finding our way back to the cars afterward isn't easy. I hold Thomasin on my lap and wave to my husband, who ends up in the second car, as we ease out of our parking space to go home.

Once there, we all pour drinks and assemble on the large screened-in porch. My younger brother Gordon, the middle child, is describing what it was like wind surfing at Cape Hatteras with Tom, who at 27 is still "the baby." He looks around the room for Tom's confirmation of his story.

"Hey, where *is* Tom?" he asks.

We all look at my mother, who shrugs, "Wasn't he in your car?" she asks my father.

"No. Wasn't he in yours?" He looks at my brother-in-law, who shakes his head.

We check the bathrooms and call up the stairs. In the confusion and darkness, Tom has apparently been left behind at the fireworks. Gordon volunteers to drive back into town to find him.

"I hate to say this," my husband says, smiling broadly at my mother, "but if you only had one child, things like this wouldn't happen."

The dinner table: 1963. Even though my mother is sitting right next to me, I have to pull on her sleeve to get her attention.

"Ma," I say, "Ma!"

"Gordon, did you finish your homework?" she asks, dishing out mashed potatoes to my younger sister, Cindy.

"Meatloaf again?" my father rolls his eyes toward the ceiling. "Can you believe it? I just had meatloaf for lunch!"

"Ma!" I say, tapping my frosted fingernails on her blue plastic placemat.

"How am I supposed to know what you had for lunch?" my mother replies, exasperated. This isn't the first time she's unwittingly duplicated my father's lunch menu.

"It doesn't matter. I'll eat it anyway." My father bows his head in resignation.

"Ma! I gotta' tell you something."

"Sherrie, you're supposed to babysit for Bunny Dockrell this weekend. I told her you were free." My older sister nods, the corona of wire-mesh rollers in her hair making her small, neat features look even more perfect.

"You know, just once I'd like to come home to a nice corned beef. And succotash. Maybe some tapioca pudding for dessert. Did any of my daughters make me tapioca?" my father asks.

"Mom. *Mother*," I say.

"Will someone please pass me the butter?" My father has lapsed into his dejected, what's-the-use-of-trying voice.

"What time does Bunny want me?" Sherrie says.

"Seven o'clock. She'll pick you up." By now the food has been served clockwise around the long table and my mother is settling down to eat her own meal. "Did it every occur to you," she asks my father, "to call me after lunch and tell me what you had to eat?"

"Call you! Call you *on the phone?*" my father snorts. "How can I possibly get through? Yak yak yak, that's all you do all day. What's the point of calling? Butter please."

"Mom! I gotta' tell you what happened to Etta." Marietta Harrison was my best friend.

"In a minute, dear. Someone please pass your father the butter."

"Mom! Gordie just stole the roll off my plate!" Cindy's ten-year-old face is a caricature of outrage. "It was the last roll!"

"Gordon! How many times do I have to tell you not to take food from other people's plates?"

"Butterplease." My father, sotto voce.

"But she already had a roll, and I haven't had any!" Gordon whines.

"Then divide the roll in half and give half of it to your sister."

It is at about this point that it starts: my father's soft drumbeat, in a low voice at first, then accompanied by a rapid, sequential tapping of his fingernails on the formica tabletop. "Buttaplease, buttaplease, bub-bub-buttaplease, buttaplease, buttaplease, bub-bub-buttaplease."

"Maaa . . ." Cindy is howling, her face scarlet all the way to the roots of her white-blond hair. "Look what he did!" She holds up a shredded fragment of roll.

"Just eat it." My mother's lips are getting thin.

My father groans, thumps his elbows on the table, and lets his head drop to his hands. "I work hard all day. You'd think once—just once—someone could do what I ask."

At this my mother gets up, taking the butter dish with her, and walks the full length of the table to deliver it to my father's place. Then she keeps right on walking—up the stairs to her room, slamming the door behind her.

My daughter is thirteen. I am driving her home from her field hockey game, which her team has just lost. Normally she does not like me to come watch her play, but because this was a big game and I pleaded with her, I was allowed to attend. Aside from taking a few photographs, I do not think I did anything to embarrass her.

"Honey, what's the homework situation tonight." I ask gently.

"Bad," is her one-word reply.

"Daddy will be home, so he can help you with your math. And you can use my computer for English."

We drive the rest of the way home in silence. When we pull into the driveway, I can see that the kitchen windows are already steamed up, and that my husband is busy preparing our dinner.

"Hey babe!" he greets her, "how'd the game go?"

"We sucked," she replies.

"We *what* ?!" I remind her.

"We sucked," she repeats. "The whole team sucked."

I let the language issue go, because I know that she is tired and depressed about the game. "Why don't you feed the cats, and then get right down to your homework?" I suggest. Then I turn to my husband. "How much longer until we eat?"

"Ten minutes," he says.

"In that case, why don't you set the table and wash your hands—after you feed the cats, that is."

"No." It is her favorite refrain these days.

"What do you mean, 'No'? No I won't feed the cats, No I won't set the table, or No I won't do my homework?" I am less confused than I pretend to be.

"Just *No*," she says, hurling her heavy backpack, hockey stick, shin pads, and grass-stained sweatshirt in a thunderous heap in the middle of the dining room floor.

"Thomasin." When I am irritated, I can compress all three syllables in her name to a single hiss. "Just *do* what I *say*."

She feeds the cats noisily, banging the cans down on the kitchen counter, letting the electric can opener make five or six unnecessary circuits, slamming the silverware drawer shut with her hip. My husband and I roll our eyes knowingly.

During dinner we dig unsuccessfully for information about her day. Did she get her math test back yet? Did she ask Mrs. Dixon for extra help in French? Are Lisa and Seth still going out?

She pushes her spaghetti aimlessly around her plate until I can stand it no longer. "Thomasin, your father and I are trying to speak to you. We want to know how your day was. We want to know what's going on in school."

"We want to know what we're paying eight thousand dollars a year for," my husband chimes in, pointing to the bill from the school accounting office on the sideboard.

"My day was terrible. Mr. Williams yelled at me for helping Ashley with her homework. My teeth were killing me. The coach made me play defense and that's probably why we lost." At the end of this extended speech a dollop of drool escapes her mouth and slides on its string to the table, where she swipes at it with an ink-stained sleeve. It really isn't her fault, I remind myself. She is still wearing a rapid palate expander. Besides, I am determined not to get into an argument.

"Honey, you played an important role in that game, even if you didn't get a chance to score. Making goals isn't everything, you know." I remind her.

"Yes it is," her father says.

"Hush," I admonish him. "Who asked you?"

"That's right, nobody asks me anything. I'm not even allowed to watch her play. Then she walks in the door and expects to be waited on hand and foot. Look at this dinner I made—she won't even eat it!"

"Jeez, Dad, chill." It is an expression we detest. "Look—I'm eating, okay?"

And so she is, speckling her uniform shirt with tomato sauce as the long strands of spaghetti flail wildly on their way to the rapid palate expander.

After dinner we all sit together in the living room near the wood stove. I am adjusting the buttons on her field hockey skirt; my husband is scanning the Britannica to find out what is the deepest lake in the world—a question for which she'll receive extra credit in geography. As bedtime draws near and the memory of the game fades, she begins to act more like our daughter.

"Mom, could you take me up to bed tonight?" Her fear of the dark has inexplicably returned in recent months. "And could you read me something short?"

From her book of fables, I read her "The Bad Kangaroo," about a poorly behaved young marsupial whose school principal comes to his house to talk to his parents. After sitting on thumbtacks concealed in the sofa by the kangaroo father, being hit by one of the mother's spitballs, and finding himself stuck to the doorknob by a blob of glue as he tries to make his escape, the principal begins to understand where the young kangaroo's behavior is coming from. The moral glares at me from the bottom of the page: *A child's conduct will reflect the ways of his parents.*

If I chose my fable unwisely, at least she is too exhausted to call me on it. I close the book and lean over to turn out her bedside light. I lie there for several minutes in the darkness, trying to put a constructive spin on the day's events. Then I ease my way off the bed.

"Are you leaving?" she asks, her voice already husky with sleep.

"Night-night, lovey," I kiss her on the forehead, which tastes like Noxema. "You're my best girl."

"I'm your *only* girl," she reminds me. And then, as I step out into the hallway, "Hey Mom?"

I pause. "Yes honey?"

"Could you leave the hall light on until you and Dad go to bed?"

The Fourth of July, 1993. It is barely a carload that attends the fireworks in Concord this year: myself, my parents, my daughter, and two of my teenage nieces. Divorce and distance have taken their toll.

It is a classic summer evening, the sky a wash of pink, the moon as translucent as beach-glass. The girls are quick to disappear: my nieces, who go to school in Concord, are anxious not to be seen with their grandparents and middle-aged aunt. So, after cautioning them about returning before darkness sets in, we watch them head off into the crowd of young people.

I spread out the old army blanket my father has always kept in the trunk of his car, and sit with my parents staring in the direction of the high school football field. We talk briefly about my daughter, the hormonal storms that have swirled about her this part year. Although I know that her behavior falls well within the normal range for a girl her age, early adolescence has already been hard on us. I ask my mother whether I gave her such trouble at thirteen.

"No, I don't ever remember having problems like that with any of you girls. I had a few problems with your brother Tom, but of course by the time he turned 13, the rest of you were out of the house and he was more like an only child."

I have been waiting for this. "Maybe you were just too distracted by having four other children."

My mother sighs. "Oh, I don't know. I just don't remember any of you every giving us a hard time. Do you, honey?" My father, who is staring at the sky, shakes his head as if he doesn't possess a single memory of our childhood.

"Mom, that's just not possible!" I protest. "How can you have five children and not remember a single bad thing about their adolescence?"

"Just lucky, I guess." My mother has that beatific look on her face that she often gets when she reflects upon the great good fortune and perfection of her life.

A sudden dull explosion, a sucking sound as the first rocket is lit, and a high-pitched whine as it rides a tight spiral skyward. My mother draws her breath in sharply, as if she has never been to the fireworks before in her life, then lets it out in a prolonged *o o o h* as a bright gold chrysanthemum spreads across the night sky. We all shift on the blanket so we can lie down with our hands folded behind our heads.

In a few days I will be 45 years old. I am alone with my parents on a blanket my father brought home from the War. I know that I was wanted from the moment of my conception. I also know that I have not disappointed them; I have married and had a child. I have followed, to the best of my ability, in their footsteps. The sky is beginning to turn a deep indigo, and the smoke from the fireworks lingers and drifts in puffs. What I am suffering through now with my own daughter is so small, so unimportant, that I too will be unable to remember it some day.

In the noise and spectacle of the display, we forget all about the three girls. They do not come back to the blanket before dark as we asked them to do, but somehow this fails to arouse our concern. Perhaps it is because, for the moment at least, our family seems complete, and we bask in the light that swells the sky before breaking into a shower of stars.

THE SECOND CHILD

Anna Quindlen

The second child was a year old yesterday. He is everything I wanted to be as a child: fearless, physical, blond. He takes no prisoners. He has also changed my life. Before him, we were two adults and a child they both adored. With him, we are a family. There is no going back.

I had a crisis of confidence when the second child was, quite literally, on the way. We were timing contractions and watching *Bachelor Party* on cable TV when I was felled by the enormity of what we had done. As a textbook-case eldest child—a leader, a doer, a convincing veneer of personality and confidence atop a bottomless pit of insecurity and need—I suspected we were about to shatter the life of the human being we both loved best in the world. We were about to snatch away his solitary splendor. Worse still, to my mind, we were about to make some unsuspecting individual a second child, a person whose baby clothes would be mottled with banana stains the first time he ever wore them, who would have a handful of photographs scattered amidst the painstaking documentation of his brother's life. An also-ran. A runner-up. "This is the heir, and that is the spare," the Duchess of Marlborough once said of her two sons.

The second child came prepared. He had a true knot in his cord, and it was wrapped around him three times, so that he emerged looking like a kidnap victim. It turned out he was feisty and winning, intrusive and alert. His character (not to mention his yellow hair) demanded clothes of his own. He clamored for the camera. He knew what he was doing. More important, so did I. The first child got me shiny new, like a new pair of shoes, but he got the blisters, too. The second child got me worn, yes, but comfortable. I told the first child I would never go away, and lied. I told the second child I would always come back, and spoke the truth. The second child had a mother who knew that the proper response to a crying baby was not to look up "Crying, causes of" in the index of Dr. Spock. As a matter of fact, he had a mother who was too busy to read childcare books at all, and so was in no position to recognize whether his "developmental milestones" were early/late/all/none of the above.

What had I expected of the first child? Everything. Rocket scientist. Neurosurgeon. Designated hitter. We talked wisely at cocktail parties about the sad mistake our mothers had made in pinning all their hopes and dreams on us. We were full of it.

I have always been a great believer in birth order. I will chat with someone for fifteen minutes and suddenly lunge at them: "You're an oldest child, aren't you?" That means something specific to me, about facing the world and facing yourself. My husband is also an oldest child, and the slogan one of his brothers coined for him is instructive: either pope or president. Not in words but in sentiment, my siblings felt the same about me. A substantial part of my character arises from such expectations.

I worried about that with the second child, worried that the child called Number One would always be so. During my second pregnancy, when I drank a bit of wine and forgot to count my grams of protein, I wondered if I was being more relaxed—or simply careless.

When I went into labor with the first, I sat down and wrote my thoughts in the beginning of his baby book. With the second, I went to a barbecue next door and then put the first to bed. The elder son was born with considerable pain, manhandled into the world with those great silver salad spoons called forceps, and when he was laid in my arms by the nurse, he looked like a stranger to me. The second somersaulted onto the birthing room bed, and as I reached down to lift him to my breast, I said his name: "Hello, Christopher." And as I saw his face, like and yet not like his brother's, I suddenly realized that wine or no wine, he had arrived with a distinct advantage. He came without baggage, after I had gotten over all the nonsense about in-utero exposure to music, and baby massage, and cloth vs. disposable diapers. What a wonderful way to be born.

And so it has occurred to me often in the last year that I must strive to give our elder son some of those things that in the usual course of events come to the younger ones. I worry less now about the second being an also-ran than I do about the first being the kind of rat-race marathon runner that birth order, in part, made me. The saddest thing I always imagined about the second child was that we would have no hopes and dreams for him. I was wrong. What he has taught us is that we will have hopes and dreams, and he will decide whether he is willing to have anything to do with them. I accept him. Perhaps in other times, or with other people, that might mean settling for less. I like to think that in his case it means taking advantage of more.

Perhaps it means that I will not push him when he needs to be pushed. I hope not. And perhaps it means I will push my first child—whose each succeeding year and stage will be inaugurals for me—when I should not do so. One teaches me as we go along, and the other inevitably reaps the benefits of that education. Each child has a different mother—not better, not worse, just different. My greatest hope and dream now is that, taken together, these two ends will make me find a middle ground in myself from which I will be happy to observe them—neither pope nor president nor obsessively striving to be either, but simply two people, their own selves, making allowances for me.

FROM THE TEMPLE OF LONGING

Roger Weingarten

The moment the children climb
into my ex-wife's car they buckle
themselves into a faraway look.
The little one
never cries, the eldest
counts white hairs that sneak
like the future up the side of his arm.
Camel, tent, oasis, storm—their ancestors
longed to pause and longed even more
to press on. But on a cobalt dark
night like this, following
an invisible need at the other
end of a leash, I want to hear
from my wild nomads dreaming
on the other side of the state. I want
to hear them say papa, it's alright,
don't cry—always thirsty at three a.m.
for something more than water. Maybe
you think this is all about a dime-

a-dozen emotional flotsam who left a furious
marriage only to miss his children from one
school holiday to the next, who exaggerates
the tangled heartworms that pressed
his ribcage when his
parents divorced. Maybe you just
want to tell me that children
are not that fragile. But I wonder
what I would hear, a dozen
years from now, waiting for the last
solar eclipse of the century, my arms relaxed
around my teenage boys, hovering
over a jerryrigged
cardboard theater, watching
the little moon erase the little sun—
I wonder what they would say
in that strange light, if I asked them
to remember.

HOMECOMING

Andrea M. Wren

I

after 45 years
of writing letters
& calling, Estelle sent word
to find a contractor—
she wants a home
built next to her sister

the house, brick & modern,
is an oddity—
sits prominently among shotgun houses,
cows, chickens, fish ponds, bait shops
& trailer homes

Celeste walks the clay red road

to see her Oakland-California-sister—
they have forty-five years to catch up on

II

Estelle & Celeste talk of the other two sisters
who died in their early 70s—
bring out boxes of black & white worn photos

Estelle rakes arthritic fingers
through Celeste's hair

conjuring memory
she parts the white/yellow-stained strands—
braids her sister's hair.

THE DEATHS OF THE UNCLES

Maxine Kumin

I am going backward in a home movie.
The reel stutters and balks before it takes hold
but surely these are my uncles spiking the lemonade
and fanning their girls on my grandmother's veranda.
My uncles, innocent of their deaths, swatting
the shuttlecock's white tit in the Sunday
twilight. Some are wearing gray suede spats, the
buttons glint like money. Two are in checkered knickers,
the bachelor uncle in his World War One puttees
is making a mule jump for the cavalry, he is crying
Tuck, dam you, Rastus, you son of a sea cook!
How full of family feeling they are, their seven
bald heads coming back as shiny as an infection,
coming back to testify like Charlie Chaplin,
falling down a lot like Laurel and Hardy.
Stanley a skeleton rattling his closet knob
long before he toppled three flights with Parkinson's.
Everyone knew Miss Pris whom he kept in rooms
over the movie theater, rooms full of rose water

while his wife lay alone at home like a tarnished
    spoon.
Mitchell the specialist, big bellied, heavy of nose,
broad as a rowboat, sniffed out the spices.
Shrank to a toothpick after his heart attack,
fasted on cottage cheese, threw out his black cigars
and taken at naptime died in his dressing gown
tidy in paisley wool, old pauper thumb in his mouth.
Jasper, the freckled, the Pepsodent smiler,
cuckold and debtor, ten years a deacon
stalled his Pierce Arrow smack on a railroad track
while the twins in their pram cried for a new father.
The twins in their pram as speechless as puppies.
O run the film forward past Lawrence the baby,
the masterpiece, handsomest, favorite issue.
Cover the screen while the hats at his funeral
bob past like sailboats, like black iron cooking pots.
Larry the Lightheart dead of a bullet.
And pass over Horace, who never embezzled,

moderate Horace with sand in his eyelids
so we can have Roger again, the mule trainer
crying *son of a sea cook!* into his dotage,
wearing the Stars and Stripes next to his hearing aid,
shining his Mason's ring, fingering his Shriner's pin,
Roger the celibate, warrior, joiner

but it was Dan Dan Dan the apple of my girlhood
with his backyard telescope swallowing the stars,
with the reedy keening of his B-flat licorice stick,
Dan who took me teadancing at the Adelphia Club.
Dan who took me boating on the Schuylkill scum.
Dan who sent the roses, the old singing telegrams
and cracked apart at Normandy leaving behind
a slow-motion clip of him leading the conga line,
his white bucks in the closet and a sweet worm in my heart.

APPROPRIATE AFFECT

Sue Miller

Grandma Frannie was a tall, slim woman, stooped now, who had been pretty before all her children were born. She still had a beautiful smile, with all her own teeth. It was sweet and sad, perhaps even reproachful, and she had used it for years to shame the family into orderly compliance. She had met Henry Winter before she finished library school, and brought to her marriage all the passion she had once lavished on the Dewey decimal system. In passion, she was disappointed. Henry was a rigid and unimaginative man, though a dutiful lover. She was pregnant within two months of the wedding, and within five years she had four daughters, Maggie, Laura, Frieda and Martha.

No one escaped the bright beam of Grandma Frannie's love. At eighty-six, she still sent birthday presents to every grandchild and great-grandchild. She remembered who was married to whom, and even who was living with whom, what his name was, and what he did. Although it didn't really matter what anyone did. Her love leapt all hurdles. Her oldest grandson, Martin, who had a coming out party within a month of moving to San Francisco, had dedicated his first volume of poetry to Frannie. His mother cried when he told her he'd sent Frannie a copy, but Frannie kept it in plain view, on the coffee table in the living room. When Martin's mother saw it there, she didn't comment. She figured Frannie probably didn't even know what it was about. And the Christmas after Fred showed up at a family Thanksgiving party with a black stripper, Frannie sent a card that brought love "to that pretty Tanya" and a gift (small, because she wasn't family) from the church bazaar.

"Christ," said Louisa, Frieda's youngest and a graduate student in psychology, "you can't be a black sheep in this family even if you want." It was true. The steady pressure of Grandma's love reduced them all, eventually, to gray normality. Even Julian, who was in prison in Joliet, Illinois, for forgery, wrote her regularly.

Frannie and Henry lived in Connecticut in a large frame house built on a hill. It had once overlooked an abandoned orchard where wizened little apples grew. Ten years before, a developer had leveled the field and built row on row of identical two-story gray town houses with fake mansard roofs.

Henry and Frannie's house was a faded salmon pink that was gently peeling, and here and there a shutter had fallen off and never been replaced. It was darkened by overgrown cedars in the front yard which reached above the roof for sunlight. The front porch listed slightly, but Bob Hancock, Laura's son-in-law, had jumped up and down on it and it held. It was pronounced safe for Frannie and Henry for the time being.

All the children wanted them to move to the retirement community nearby, but Henry couldn't bear

to think of it. He loved the ornate woodwork and soot-streaked wallpaper, the dark furniture inherited from his mother, and the threadbare Oriental rugs.

One Sunday afternoon, an hour or so after their return from the Congregational church, Henry was watching football on television. Frannie came into the living room to tell him that dinner was ready. It was in the middle of the third quarter and that irritated Henry. Because he was slightly deaf and had the television on loud, he didn't hear her coming and that irritated him even more. She stepped suddenly into his line of vision and turned the set off. She shouted, "Dinner, Henry," at him, and smiled her warm, browbeaten smile.

Henry stood up. "There's no need to shout," he said. "What's more, I'm not ready for dinner and I won't be for a good long while. The Sabbath was made for man, madam, not man for the Sabbath." And he walked right over to the TV set and turned it back on.

She said something to him, but he ignored her, so she started her long, slow shuffle back to the kitchen.

Henry turned the set off about forty-five minutes later and started toward the kitchen himself. His walk was brisker and more steady than Frannie's. He stopped abruptly when he rounded the doorway to the dining room. Frannie's legs were sticking straight out from behind the highboy on the floor. He felt a numbed panic as he approached her. She was sitting up, wedged in the corner between the highboy and the wall. Her face was white and agonized. Her mouth had dropped open and her eyes were closed.

"My dear!" Henry said, bending over her stiffly from the waist. He saw her lips move slightly as though she were trying to talk. Her left arm rested uselessly on the floor and her right was somehow bent behind her. Henry reached down and tried to lift her up, but he only managed to slide her forward slightly. Her head lolled back and smacked the wall. Henry cried out. He straightened and started into the kitchen. Halfway to the telephone, with his arms already lifting to take off the receiver and dial, he turned and went back to her. He bent down again.

"I'll be right back, my darling," he said very loudly and clearly, as though she were the deaf one. She made no sign that she'd heard. He went back and placed the call.

·　　·　　·

No one answered when the ambulance driver rang the bell, so the men walked in with the stretcher. They looked around the dark, empty front hall and then heard a murmuring voice from the room on their right, the dining room. Henry had pulled a chair over next to Frances, and he was sitting in it, holding her hand across his knees and patting it, talking softly to her.

When the ambulance driver was only a few steps away, Henry saw him and stopped talking. He stood up. "Sir, my name is Henry Winter and this is my wife," he said. He began to explain the circumstances under which he'd found her, but the men were already lifting her onto the stretcher and strapping her in, giving loud instructions to each other.

"You coming in the ambulance, Pop?" the driver asked as he picked up his end of the stretcher.

"What say?" asked Henry, turning his head so his good ear was nearer the driver.

"Are you coming with us?" the driver yelled.

"Ah! Much obliged, but I'll follow in my car," said Henry, and he want to get his hat and coat.

"Christ!" the driver said a minute later as they hoisted Frannie into the truck. "Can you imagine them letting an old guy like that have a license?"

In the days following Frannie's stroke, different children, grandchildren and great-grandchildren came and went in the house. As though it were an old country hotel getting ready for the season, rooms that had been shut up for years were opened, mouse droppings and dead insects were swept up and mattresses turned over.

Frannie's daughters ransacked the bedding box and clucked to each other about the down puffs and heavy linen sheets with hand stitching that you would think Mother might have handed down by now.

For the first three days they took turns going in one at a time to sit by Frannie in intensive care. They got permission to have a member of the family stay by her straight through the night. The third night it was her granddaughter Charlotte's turn.

The overhead lights were off in the hospital room, but a white plastic nipple plugged into the wall socket next to Frannie's bed glowed like a child's night light and Charlotte could see the shape of her grandmother's skinny body under the bedclothes. She didn't like to look at Gram's face, so embryonic and naked without her glasses, her hair uncombed for three days and her mouth slack. Instead she looked at the sac of IV fluid with its plastic umbilicus running into Gram's bruised arm. Or she held Gram's freckled hand, which lay alongside the mound of bones under the sheets; or she slept; or wept. She rubbed her hands up and down her slightly thickening waist and cried as she thought of life and death; of Gram about to die, and of the baby, her third, taking life inside her own body.

She had tried to talk about this to her younger sister, Louisa, the afternoon before at Frannie and Henry's house, but Louisa had been irritable. Louisa was always irritable when Charlotte cried. "Oh, spare us, why don't you," she'd said, chopping onions for stew. Her knife whacked the board rapidly, like a burst of gunfire. "Next you'll be going on about reincarnation."

Charlotte blew her nose loudly into a Kleenex, and wiped her lower lids carefully so the mascara wouldn't smear. Grandma Frannie stirred slightly and swung her head toward Charlotte. Her mouth closed with a smacking sound and opened again. Charlotte leaned toward the bed, grabbing the steel railings that boxed her grandmother in.

"Gram?" she whispered. She cleared her throat. "Gram?" Her grandmother's eyes snapped open and stared wildly for a second. Then the lids seemed to grow heavy and they drooped again.

Charlotte stood up and put one hand on her grandmother's shoulder. The other hand rested on her own belly. At her touch, her grandmother's eyes opened again and she frowned and seemed to try to fix Charlotte in focus with the anxious intensity of a newborn.

"Gram? Do you hear me?" Charlotte said. "Do you hear me?"

After a few seconds' pause, Grandma Frannie nodded, a slow swaying of her frizzy head.

"Do you know me?" asked Charlotte. Gram shut her lips and tightened them and frowned hard at Charlotte.

"It's Charlotte, Grandma," she said, and started to weep again. Her right hand was furiously rubbing her belly. She was already thinking of how she would tell the others of this moment. She leaned over and put her face close to her grandmother's.

"It's Charlotte, Grandma. Do you know me?"

Again her grandmother moved her head slightly, up and down. Her lips quivered with some private effort.

"Oh, Grandma, I wanted you to know. I'm going to have a baby." Tears ran down Charlotte's face and plopped on the neatly folded sheet covering her grandmother's chest. "I'm going to have another baby, Gram."

There was no change in the intense frown on Grandma Frannie's face, but her mouth opened. Charlotte leaned closer still and Grandma Frannie's breath was horrible in her face. Frannie's lips worked and her breathing was shallow and fast.

"The. Nasty. Man," she whispered.

Charlotte reported to the doctors and the family that Grandma Frannie had waked in the night and had spoken. When they asked, as they did eagerly and repeatedly, what she had said, Charlotte would only say that she hadn't been herself. Her cousin Elinore thought Charlotte was being "a bit of a snot" not to tell, trying to rivet all that attention on herself. Charlotte felt everyone's irritation with her all the next day. Frannie was fluttering delicately in and out of consciousness and muttered only incoherent phrases as the nurses changed her bedding or inserted another IV. But Charlotte still tearfully refused to tell what it was Grandma had said to her, although she insisted that Grandma had spoken clearly. "God, you'd think it was her mantra," Louisa said.

After Charlotte heard Grandma Frannie speak, the family came by twos and threes for several days. Slowly Frannie began to recognize them, calling out their names as they walked in. Sometimes she couldn't seem to say the name and then she'd spell it aloud, carefully and often correctly. It was a small hospital, and the doctors and nurses came to know the family as they sat in little clusters in the lounge or cafeteria, waiting for a turn to see Frannie.

In the evening at the house, there were always nine or ten around the dinner table. Henry felt an almost unbearable joy sometimes when he was called in to the extended table covered with a white linen cloth. The china and glassware glittered. The tureens and platters that had come down from his parents were heaped with food like creamed onions and scalloped potatoes, food Henry hadn't eaten at home in years, except at Thanksgiving or Christmas.

They talked animatedly at the table of what Gram had said or done that day. Everyone had a favorite story he liked to tell. Frannie had asked Elinore to get the bedpan, but called it a perambulator. She had clearly asked Maggie if she was going to die and cried when Maggie told her she would not, that she was getting better. She rambled on and on to Emily, her youngest grandchild, who was down from Smith for the weekend. She talked about apple trees and she had said, "I think of all those trees gone, don't you know, the apples, all cut down. Well, that's the way. All those trees." Emily had sat in the darkened room and stroked her hand. "Why would they do a thing like that?" Grandma Frannie had asked, and Emily had said, honestly, that she didn't know. Then Grandma Frannie had said, "Those assholes!" but Emily was sure she meant to say "apples," so she didn't repeat that part.

Henry told over and over how he had found her and called for the ambulance. He didn't tell the whole truth. He said, "My dearest was in the kitchen making dinner. I sat in the corner of the living room, you see, watching football—it was, I believe, the Los Angeles Rams that day, but I could be wrong—and when the game was over, I walked back towards the kitchen to inquire about dinner, and as I came around the corner, what do you think I saw?" He would wait here however long it took some listener to ask, "What?"

"*There* was my darling sitting on the floor with her legs protruding out from behind the highboy that Auntie gave us for a wedding present." He would go on, detailing every step of the process of getting Frannie to the hospital, and making himself sound very heroic.

The group staying at the house shrank and stabilized somewhat after it became clear that Frannie was going to survive. Maggie stayed on with Henry to take care of him, and Charlotte, who lived nearby, often came for part of the day while her children were in school. Sometimes she returned later with them and her husband, to have dinner with Maggie and Henry.

Frequently, one of the other children or grandchildren would arrive for a day or two. Michael stopped in one night with his entire band, Moonshot, and a few of their girlfriends on the way to a gig in the Berkshires. Maggie told everyone later, "Who knows who was with whom. I just told them where the bedrooms were and shut my eyes."

Grandma Frannie made extraordinary progress. She was having therapy with a walker and physically she had recovered almost completely, except for a dragging in her left leg. Most of her powers of speech had returned. But she still had trouble with an occasional word and when she was tired she would lose track of where she was and to whom she was speaking and drift off to other places and times. Like a baby, she napped three or four times a day.

One afternoon, Henry went in alone to visit her. She was asleep. Her mouth puffed out with each exhalation and she snored faintly. Henry stood in the open doorway and tried to engage some of the passing hospital staff in conversation. His loud voice woke Frannie up.

"Henry!" she called to him.

He turned. "Oh, my dear, now you're awake, and looking so well today, so very well." He leaned over and kissed her cheek.

"Graphics," she said.

"Eh?"

She bit her lip and looked angry. "Now I didn't mean that," she said. "Fetch me my . . . you know." She pointed to her nose. The marks of her glasses were like permanent bluish stains on either side of the bridge. "They're somewhere or other in that coffin there," and she gestured at the stand by her bed.

Henry opened the drawer and got her glasses out. He started to help her put them on, but she waved his hands away and hooked them over her ears herself.

"My love," Henry began, seating himself by her bed. But she cut him off. "Where *were* you?" she asked.

"Why, my dear, I just arrived, but you were asleep so I stood by the door. . . ."

"Not likely!" she snapped, and behind her glasses her eyes glinted malevolently at him.

"Very well, my love," he said in an injured tone, resolved to be patient. The doctors had told him it was a miracle she had survived at all, and besides, Henry couldn't forget the shame of his behavior to her in the moments before her stroke. Worse yet, he found himself hoping she would never recover fully enough to recall it herself, to blame him or tell the children.

"I heard you down there in that other room," Frannie said, slowly and carefully.

"Now, Frannie, you must stay calm."

She shut her eyes and seemed for a moment to relax or to be asleep. Then her eyes opened and she smiled. "Yes, I'm not well. Not a bit well."

"But you're getting better."

Her lips labored, as through choosing the exact position they needed to be in to form the next word. "The children were here."

"That's right, dear."

"Maggie. And Frieda. And Martha. And that other."

"Laura? She couldn't come. She wasn't here."

"Not Laura," she said irritably. "Not one of mine. That other."

"Louisa? Charlotte?"

"Yes! That one." She smiled in satisfaction. A moment later she said, "Did I tell you the children were here?"

"Yes, you just did, my love. You just said that." And he laughed loudly at her.

Her eyes narrowed behind the bifocals. Her mouth tensed into an angry line. A nurse walked in briskly.

"Ah, here comes that . . ." She stopped.

"It's Nurse Gorman, Mrs. Winter. Just checking your blood pressure again."

"Again? You have nothing superior to do?" Something funny in her sentence made Frannie shake her head angrily.

"I just wanted to get another reading 'cause it's been a few hours, honey." She pumped up the band around Frannie's skinny arm, squeezing the loose flesh close to the bone. "Your wife is my favorite patient, Mr. Winter. She's a doll."

"Eh?" said Henry.

"Your wife is doing well," yelled the nurse. She was tall and wore glasses and very red lipstick.

"Oh, I know, yes, thanks," said Henry.

After the nurse left, Frannie closed her eyes for a while and seemed to sleep again. Henry looked at a copy of *Newsweek* he'd picked up in the lobby.

"Oh, you're still here." She labored over the words.

"Yes, my love," he said, and patted her hand.

"Why don't you just go down there. If you want to. Go right on down. To your little nurse."

Henry frowned.

"I heard you down there. Yes. The children, probably. Thought it was just me again. Making that noise. But I knew just what it was with that Mrs. Sheffield." She said this very slowly and precisely. "Fuck-ing Mrs. Sheffield."

Henry started and withdrew his hand.

"Always that. Mrs. Sheffield. When I wanted some other nurse, but oh, no, you had to have her. Again. Sneaking off down the hall. Did you think I couldn't hear? You? I knew just what it was. I heard you."

"You're upset, Frances. You—you should sleep."

"Yes. Sleep. Don't you wish. I saw you looking at her. As soon as I sleep you'll go off. Down the hall again. Why couldn't we have some other nurse? I didn't want Mrs. Sheffield again." Her voice had become plaintive.

Henry stood up.

Frances began to cry. Her face crumpled into bitter lines. "I don't want her. There's too many children here, and you. Always sneaking around with her, making those noises down the hall. Yes, go. Go on. I know where you're . . . you're going."

Henry drove home slowly. He didn't notice the line of cars forming behind him and he didn't hear the honking. The sun was low and pink in the Connecticut sky. He was remembering Mrs. Sheffield, whose eyes had bulged out slightly so that the whites showed all the way around the iris and made Henry think of nipples sitting round and staring in the middle of her breasts. She was quiet and solemn as she performed her duties after Maggie's birth and she wouldn't sit with him at meals. He had known what he wanted from her when he wrote to hire her again for the second child. After that she had come and stayed with them at each birth, and Frannie, he thought, had never known. Mrs. Sheffield was small and plump, with dark hair, and he had been right, her nipples did sit exactly in the middle of her small breasts, unlike his wife's, which drooped down and leaked milk at his mouth's pull for years on end.

When he got home, Henry called the doctor and explained that he thought his presence was distressing to his wife, and with his permission Henry wouldn't come in for a bit. The doctor was surprised that Henry thought he needed permission to stay away.

And now each person who visited Frannie came to a point in telling how she was doing where he or she would fall silent and then say in a perplexed tone that Grandma Frannie was still not really herself. In little groups of two and three they discussed her and they agreed that they wouldn't have believed Grandma Frannie even knew the meaning of half the words she was using. She told Charlotte's husband that Henry didn't know the first thing about fucking. She said "fucking." "In and out," she said. "That was his big idea. I hope you take a little more time and care. And if you don't know what's up," she said, "there's no shame in asking."

She told Maggie that she had thought she would die when they were all little. She said she'd spent fifteen years "up to my elbows in runny yellow shit. Not one of you children turned out a well-formed stool until you were doing it on your own."

Maggie had blushed and spoken to her as though she were a child. "Be nice, Mother," she'd said, nervously smiling.

"Oh, nice, nice!" said Grandma Frannie. "I know very well how to be nice."

Like Henry, the children and grandchildren began to think of reasons why they couldn't visit. Maggie still went once a day, but most of the time the others stayed away. Late one night Maggie called her husband long-distance in Pennsylvania. She stood in her flannel nightgown in the hall and sobbed softly into the phone so Henry wouldn't hear her. "I can't imagine where she ever heard that kind of language. I almost wished she'd died rather than end up like this."

A few weeks after this, when Frannie began to get better, the doctors called it the return of "appropriate affect." Maggie sent out a family letter saying: "Mother's coming around. She's practically back to normal except for forgetting a few words and we're planning on a homecoming party soon."

And later: "Mother seems just about okay now. Sends her love to everyone and asks about you all. She can't remember who visited and who didn't, but she's talking normally now, thank goodness. For those who can come, we'll bring her home February 16 in the early afternoon and the doctor says a very short party would be all right."

Snow had fallen the night of the fifteenth, but the sixteenth was bright and cold. Frannie's daughters and granddaughters took charge of lunch. One of the sons-in-law put the extra leaf in the table again and took three of the smaller children out to shovel the walk. They ran in and out all morning, bringing cold air and snow into the front hall. "Here, here," Henry said crossly. "In or out. I'm not paying to heat all outdoors."

Someone brought a towel and left it by the front door to mop up the puddles of melting snow. Charlotte's husband lugged two high chairs up from the basement, washed off the dust and cobwebs, and set them at corners of the table.

The chime of the metal shovel ringing on concrete outside, the banging of the front door, the good smells from the kitchen, the table gleaming with silver, made it seem like a dozen Christmases they'd shared in the past. But there was a subdued anxiousness among the adults and several tense abbreviated conversations. Maggie said over and over to people, "Really, she's quite all right now." Henry was surly and spent the morning watching TV or scolding his great-grandchildren.

At one o'clock, Bob Hancock's car swung up the driveway. His oldest boy, Nick, jumped out from the far side and extracted a walker from the back seat. He brought it around to the door Bob was opening at the foot of the walk. Frannie rose slowly out of the car and Nick put the walker down in front of his great-grandmother. The children who were outside danced around her and their muffled shouts brought the family in the house to the windows. "She's home! She's home!" they cried. Henry rose and went to the window.

Slowly, with Nick at one elbow and Bob at the other, Frannie made her way across the shoveled, sanded walk.

Her entourage of great-grandchildren in bright nylon snowsuits leapt around her. She was watching her feet, so Henry couldn't see her face. Charlotte had gone to the hospital two days before to give her a permanent, and her hair was immobilized in rigid waves on her head, though the wind made her coat flap.

She turned at the bottom of the porch stairs and Bob came to face her. Holding each other's hands like partners in some old court dance, they stepped sideways up the stairs. Then the children burst open the front door, yelling and stomping the snow off their feet and taking advantage of the excitement to dance around in the front hall without having to remove their boots. Frannie shuffled in and looked around at her family gathered in an irregular circle in the hallway. Charlotte fished a Kleenex out of her maternity smock and several others wiped at their eyes.

"Where's Henry?" Frannie asked. Henry felt a slight constriction in his chest, but he pushed past his children and grandchildren and stood before her. "Here I am, my darling," he said. She looked at him a moment. Then she smiled her sad smile and raised her face to be kissed. Gratefully, he put his lips to hers.

The children yelled and danced, the adults broke into applause. Henry said softly, "It's wonderful to see you yourself again, Frances."

Grandma Frannie looked at him and then at her clapping family. She raised her hands slightly as though to ward off the noise, and for a moment her face registered confusion. But the applause continued.

Then she seemed to realize what they wanted from her. Unassisted and shaky, she stepped forward and smiled again. Slowly she bowed her head, as though to receive the homage due a long and difficult performance.

WHAT I LEARNED FROM MY MOTHER

Julia Kasdorf

I learned from my mother how to love
the living, to have plenty of vases on hand
in case you have to rush to the hospital
with peonies cut from the lawn, black ants
still stuck to the buds. I learned to save jars
large enough to hold fruit salad for a whole
grieving household, to cube home-canned pears
and peaches, to slice through maroon grape skins
and flick out the sexual seeds with a knife point.
I learned to attend viewings even if I didn't know
the deceased, to press the moist hands
of the living, to look in their eyes and offer

sympathy, as though I understood loss even then.
I learned that whatever we say means nothing,
what anyone will remember is that we came.
I learned to believe I had the power to ease
awful pains materially like an angel.
Like a doctor, I learned to create
from another's suffering my own usefulness, and once
you know how to do this, you can never refuse.
To every house you enter, you must offer
healing: a chocolate cake you baked yourself,
the blessing of your voice, your chaste touch.

THE BROWN PATCH

Paul Martin

For Kenny, my foster son

Looking through the rain-streaked window
at the budding trees, the grass turning green,
I see the brown patch you wore in the lawn
bouncing the rubber ball off the house
back to yourself.
From inside it sounded like the thump
of an insistent heart.
Was ours the third house? I can't remember,
But the day they took you back
we sat in enormous chairs at opposite
ends of the front room, a plain growing between us.

I held you as close as I could
then watched you carry your suitcase
out to the waiting car.
Now, two years later, I try to imagine
what we might have had, you and I,
but all I see is this brown patch
mottled with a fine, green moss.
Somedays it looks like a blind, featherless
bird fallen from its nest.
Today it's a strange, unexplored continent,
a place I know only from maps.

·

Part 3

SOUNDS THAT BOND

AFTER MAKING LOVE
WE HEAR FOOTSTEPS

Galway Kinnell

For I can snore like a bullhorn
or play loud music
or sit up talking with any reasonably sober Irishman
and Fergus will only sink deeper
into his dreamless sleep, which goes by all in one flash,
but let there be that heavy breathing
or a stifled come-cry anywhere in the house
and he will wrench himself awake
and make for it on the run—as now, we lie together,
after making love, quiet, touching along the length of
　　our bodies,
familiar touch of the long-married,
and he appears—in his baseball pajamas, it happens,
the neck opening so small
he has to screw them on, which one day may make
　　him wonder
about the mental capacity of baseball players—
and says, "Are you loving and snuggling? May I join?"
He flops down between us and hugs us and snuggles
　　himself to sleep,
his face gleaming with satisfaction at being this very
　　child.

In the half darkness we look at each other
and smile
and touch arms across his little, startlingly muscled
　　body—
this one whom habit of memory propels to the ground
　　of his making,
sleeper only the mortal sounds can sing awake,
this blessing love gives again into our arms.

THE OTHER MOTHER

Tzivia Gover

I had a ten-month-old baby girl when I began a new job. I had told my boss, an easy-going man with gray hair and a youthful gait, that I had a child. But I was vague about the rest of my family constellation. I was used to opening up slowly about my personal life, first judging just how easy-going a person really was.

One afternoon shortly after I was hired, I ran into my boss and his son at the playground. We sat at the edge of the sandbox admiring each other's children. Then I noticed mine was hungry. I scooped her up and returned to the bench near the see-saws, where my partner sat reading.

I wished she didn't have to nurse our daughter right there and then, as I didn't feel ready to "come out" to my boss. But I had already learned that with a baby around, things don't always go as planned. As he left, my boss waved to us. From the distance I couldn't get a clear reading on his reaction, but I took the lively salute as a sign of acceptance. Either way, I thought, now he knew I was a lesbian, and that our baby had two mothers.

But he didn't. At work he never asked about my partner. I assumed he was trying to be nonchalant about it. Then one day we were discussing our respective day care setups. "Looks like you've got a nice arrangement with that baby-sitter," he said.

"Baby-sitter?"

"That woman in the park."

What did he think? That my partner was a wet nurse? "John, didn't you notice she was breast-feeding our baby?" I asked.

He hadn't. That situation stuck with me. It demonstrated how people try desperately to fit what they observe into the corset of their rigid version of reality. Every child has one and only one mother, our mythology goes. The space for Mother had already been filled in my boss's mind. Therefore, even seeing my partner nursing our baby didn't alter his picture. Instead, he unconsciously, I'm sure, glossed over the piece that didn't fit.

This misunderstanding, and many more like it, taught me that if I wanted to be sure people understood who our family was, I had to be painstakingly diligent in my explanations. I also learned how strong was people's need to believe in One Mother, with the same fervor that they believe in One God, or One Nation.

To be honest, this realization was forming from the moment I learned Sophie was pregnant. I suppose all couples spend late nights, long dinners and obsessive afternoons trying to arrive at just the right name for their baby-to-be. We did that, too. But, in addition, like a very small minority of parents, we also spent hours, days, and months deciding what the child would call *me*. We had to name the other mother.

We went to the library and researched African words for mother, having heard that African cultures allow for more than one type of mother per child. We tried on different variations of the word mother: Sophie would be Mommy and I'd be Mama, or Mami. Finally, we decided that since we were Jewish, our child would call me Ima, Hebrew for mother.

I loved the idea. *Ima* was a label that let me be Tabitha's* mother in word and in deed. But the foreign word also signified that while I was Tabitha's female parent, I wasn't the same kind of mother as Sophie was. Ima was a familiar word, a word that others in our family and community would understand, but it distinguished me as a separate parent.

That wasn't the end of our name game. Now we had to decide what the rest of the world would call me. For example, would we tell the director at day care that I was Tabitha's *Ima*? Unless she was Jewish, she wouldn't understand. When both Sophie and I showed up at the doctor's and had to explain who had given birth to Tabitha, would we say, Sophie is the biological mother, and Tzivia is the co-parent?

In lesbian parenting books and articles, moms like me were referred to as the non-biological mother. But that was too sterile for my tastes. Besides, it wasn't true. I'm as biologically sound as the next mother. Co-mother,

---

* To ensure my family's privacy, I have chosen to use pseudonyms for them in this essay.

a term accepted in most liberal circles, sounded too much like co-pilot to me. I was more than just an assistant. Since other couples we knew called the parent who didn't give birth the father, I even considered that. But Sophie argued that it would be too confusing for Tabitha, and of course, I agreed.

We affectionately referred to me as "the other mother." It was descriptive after all. No one questioned that Sophie was Tabitha's mother. And as the other female parent, I was the mother, also.

But as time wore on, the label became less charming. I came to feel that referring to myself glibly as the other mother had similar overtones to a man's mistress appearing at a social function on his arm, and introducing herself as the other woman. This is something we all know happens, but for heaven's sake, let's not admit it.

Granted, lesbians choosing to begin families together is a relatively recent trend. But "other mothers" have been around in various forms forever. The child who was adopted has a birth mother and an adoptive mother. Until very recently, the birth mother was erased from the family's consciousness to make things fit.

The picture we have of these other mothers is of an irresponsible, immoral woman who was ill-behaved and had to pay the price. When a woman admits, even today, that she is going to give a baby over for adoption because she knows she can't emotionally or financially support the child, she's labeled as "cruel" or "heartless." Witness the homes for pregnant women that still exist today, where women who are going to put their children up for adoption can carry their pregnancies through in private. As a society we have no fond feelings for other mothers. It is difficult even to utter the word "step-mother" without wanting to put the adjective "evil" first.

I know lesbian couples who refer to the non-birth parent as an aunt, or simply by her first name. This despite the fact that she helped make the decision to start a family, probably even inseminated her partner with sperm from a friend or a sperm bank. And this despite the fact that she was there for the child's birth, was awake for all of the feedings, probably changing a diaper after her partner finished nursing the baby. And this despite the fact that the child knows this family member is her parent, and has probably even tried to call her "mommy" on occasion.

When I have wondered whether I have the right to call myself a mother, my child has always answered for me, even before she could speak. When Sophie was pregnant she thought we should talk to the child growing in her womb. Not being the sentimental type, I thought the idea was hokey. But I was roped in. I sat facing Sophie's abdomen and played lullabies on my flute. Each day I'd lay a hand where the baby was kicking and yell silly greetings, like "Hello, in there," as if I were calling down a rabbit hole.

When Tabitha was born Sophie and I were surrounded by two nurses, a midwife, and the baby's godmother. We were all talking at once when Tabitha first came into the world. But we noticed that her wide eyes seemed to focus selectively on Sophie and me.

She knew whose she was from the start.

CONVERSATION

John Updike

My little girl keeps talking to me.
"Why do you look so sad?" she asks,
and, "Isn't Mommy beautiful?"

As if she knows next summer she
will be too near a woman's state
to be so bold, she propositions,
"Let's run along the beach!"
So, hand in hand, we feel to fly
until as if with grains of sand
our skin turns gritty where we touch.
We flirt and giggle, driving back.

With nervous overkill of love
she comes to see me hammer
at the barn, and renders praise:
"You must be the carefullest shingler

in all the world." Indeed, I snap
the blue-chalked line
like a ringmaster's whip, and stare
in aligning the cedar butts
as if into a microscope whose slides
have sectioned the worms of my mind.

At night, guarding her treasure,
watching me frown and read, she falls
asleep, her morning-brushed hair
gone stiff like straw, her braces
a slender cage upon her humid face.
Too heavy to lift, slumped helpless
beneath the power of my paternal gaze,
her half-formed body begs,
"Don't leave. Don't leave me yet."

SILENCE IS A LOUD, LOUD LANGUAGE

Bobbie Su Nadal

Life is the first gift, love the second, and understanding the third.
—Marge Piercy

She calls, says, "Come if you can. We need to talk."

"What is it, Mother?" I ask. "Are you sick? Did you hurt yourself?"

"Don't be silly. Are you coming or not?"

Four days since the phone call, and the taxi blasts from baggage claim into the seam of bumper-to-bumper traffic, squeals onto Century Boulevard, the dark insides of the cab stuttering reflected light like a strobe from the bright billboards that line the street all the way northbound to I-405. It's been years since I've seen my mother, and now I don't know whether to ask the driver to speed up or slow down. Either way, my childhood home will appear soon enough—forty-five minutes at most, even in this unseasonable rain.

What is it with mothers and daughters anyway? It's as if my mother and I had been born in separate countries with common borders but alien alphabets. When we try to communicate, somewhere in their formation the words become bent with misunderstanding, turn into a collection of incoherent syllables. Our years together are littered with failed efforts to find a common language.

Mother is a woman of hard-honed strength, a woman born to a large German Catholic family on a small Nebraska farm, a family too busy keeping food on the table to have time to talk or listen. Their communication consisted mainly of Franklinesque proverbs, capsulized codes of conduct for the business of living: "Don't put off till tomorrow what you can do today." "If you don't have anything nice to say, don't say anything at all." That, plus a strict Church doctrine and the Ten Commandments—no one dared question the wisdom of this simple and effective system.

Mother included these codes into our own family's dialect, but in the form of parables, dizzying stories of disasters into which she wove a sequence of tenuously related subjects, half fact, half fiction, peopled with characters I did not know. They are all I remember of our early conversations. I guessed that the tales were supposed to teach me cautionary lessons, but long before I could figure out the point of the story, I would be lost among all those words. I would stare at her in bafflement until she turned away abruptly, exasperated.

As I approached adolescence, matters became worse. No longer willing to listen in helpless confusion, I would challenge her stories and their validity. Through them I felt I was challenging her values, and in essence, the parental authority that I just could not communicate with. Perhaps *this* way I could reach her, I thought, as I rushed headlong into battle. But all that happened was that her stories collapsed into an uncompromising silence.

I began to think I was a genetic mistake, a bald, blank cell that grew dull, an unsilvered mirror incapable of reflection. She could not see herself in me any more than I could see myself in her. We had nothing in common, nothing in our physical appearance, nothing in our personalities, nothing in our basic vocabularies. And so we danced a slow and tortuous dance, out and out into fragmented circles, until our alienation was complete, until all our words, spoken and unspoken, were like dried twigs under our tongues.

Adolescence is a time of pain, but it is also a naive and hopeful time. Surely when I went away to college, I believed, we would be able to start over. It would allow us the distance we needed, the time between our conversations. It would be a forced truce. It would give me the necessary skills to tell her how I felt. And so at college words became my passion. I devoured the great works of literature and memorized the vocabularies of the best orators, trying to find in them a solution to our wordlessness. In my sophomore year, I wrote a poem for Mother, hoping to articulate my deep sense of loss at our verbal impasse:

> Mother
>
> my mouth is stuffed
> with all this silence
> between us. What
> should we do with our
> wild words, the ones

that bay like dogs
outside our window
at night, that snarl
between the long teeth
of time?
They've grown bloated
over the years, soured
in the dark recesses
of our hearts where
we tried to cage them.
I hear them restless now,
multiplying in packs.
I hear them clatter sharp claws
on our bare floors, hear them
clanging at the gate.

When she received my poem, she called and said, "I didn't know they had wild dogs at school, honey. Don't forget to lock your door."

It's still raining. Muddy tracks send slanted streaks running along the back windows. I look through them for familiar road signs, see, slashed into the hips of the San Gabriel Mountains, new roads that I could never have imagined possible. I remember earlier homecom-ings, riding over the rise and seeing all the lights filling the valley like fireflies. Tonight it is dark, like looking into a decayed tooth.

After I started a family of my own, we tried again to close the gap between us. But we could speak only in courtesies. I'd call her once a week to ask if she was all right. She'd say she was "just fine, thank you." It took all of five minutes to say everything we could concerning the weather, the neighborhood, the kids, the house. We sidestepped all controversial or emotionally charged is-sues. Our language was that of polite conversation—safe, boring, comfortable—but with a dull ache underneath.

I used to visit her with my children in the fall and summer. Strangely enough, there was an immediate, wonderful connection between my daughter and mother. It pleased me to see how easy they were with one another, what pure joy phrased their simple conversa-tions. On the last visit, I handed another poem to Mother, one that I erased from my computer immedi-ately on my return but cannot remove from my own memory today:

At Dusk My Mother

sits in her mother's chair,
works the wicker rocker
and her rosary

at a peaceful pace.
She gazes outside the window
where her granddaughter
who wears her grandmother's chin,
her gold-green eyes,
rides a bike with sturdy legs
under a Chinese pistachio tree which
has burst into flame.

Time leans against
my mother. She feels it
pinch her left hip,
her right elbow,
feels it daily, the way
it chisels circles
around her eyes, her mouth.

The room grows gray.
She gathers the past on her lap
the way she used to
gather children,
presses a string of names
across the beads,
pleads a blessing
for mother, father,
husband of nearly forty years,
all gone now.

She sits and prays,
sits and smiles
at the little girl outside
glowing in the dark.

This time Mother dissolved into tears, turned and hurried into her own room, closing the door.

"What is it, Mother? Did I write something wrong? Was it the part about being old? I'm sorry if I hurt you. Please come out and talk to me."

Hours later she called me in, handed me a sealed envelope that had "Adoption Papers" printed across it. She didn't have to say a word. Instinctively, I knew they were my own. And suddenly, everything fell into place. It wasn't the part about being old, or the part about her dead loved ones. It was the part that I thought would make her happy, the part about the physical resemblance between my daughter and her that finally cut deep enough to expose the secret she had hidden all this time.

A mix of emotions flooded me: anger for the years of deceit and the wasted efforts at trying to understand her, and relief for what I thought was a simple answer to all our problems, clicking into place with the precision of a bullet sliding into its chamber. This finally was cold, clear language: we simply were not related.

We're on the Ventura Freeway at the Coldwater Canyon exit, and before I'm ready, we're at 4545. I nervously pay the driver too much. He leaves me standing in the mist, jarred by the sharp smell of wet camphor trees that rim my mother's lot. The street light is out, but I could have found my way, blindfolded, up the eleven flagstone stairs to the screened front door that still creaks when I pull it open.

I'm counting the years since our last conversation, that last confrontation. Four. No, longer, much too long.

I think of us, mother and daughter, our wounds from all that emotional rending and ripping, and know this is our last chance. I think of what to say, how to say it just right. I go over and over each sentence: how it's no longer important to me that we're not blood-related; how she's still my mother, the only one I'll ever have; how the last few years have taught me what living without her would be like; how I think we've both been stubborn for too long. . . . Then the door opens, and there, standing in the smile of the doorway in a cloud of white hair that frames her face, is Mother.

Where are they now, those fine-tuned words that I thought could change things between us, make everything OK? I can't find them. . . . She holds out her arms and we fall back into each other's life, cling to each other as though to life rafts that float easily over all our debris. Somewhere in this sweet silence, so new to us, more precious than birthright, louder than any spoken word, is forgiveness and healing.

"Mother," I say, "I'm learning to listen to our silence."

She says, "Welcome home."

DOUBLE-TAKE:
THE BILINGUAL FAMILY

Peter Wortsman

Two tongues tug at my childhood mind, two takes on the world, two flavors of consciousness.

English is the public channel of communication at school and on the street, a peppermint tongue that stings and excites. German, all chocolaty, viscous and sweet, the private funnel of intimacy in my first generation Austrian-Jewish immigrant family. And though I'm a native New Yorker, my emotional grounding is definitely in German, the dialect of that tiny city state of five afloat in the teeming megalopolis.

English means business, sharpened Number 2 pencils, white shirt and tie; commerce: "I'll trade you a Roger Maris for a Mickey Mantle!"; and diplomacy: "If you don't, I won't be your best friend anymore!"

German coddles, curses and cajoles. "Wir sind jung, die Welt ist offen!" (We are young, the world is open!) my mother invokes a song from her youth to rally the ranks at reveille and bedtime. My father fondly dubs his belly "Mein Backhändlfriedhof" (fried chicken cemetery), and us kids his "Affengesindel" (monkey mob) or "Arschgesichter" (ass faces), depending on our manners and his mood—language the like of which we wouldn't dream of using outside the home. While English calls for good behavior, German is a license to relax.

My father, who speaks seven languages and who fled the Nazis with nothing but the clothes on his back, talked his way past the Czech border guards in perfect French. "Language is a portable treasure, a lifeline," he insists. Other fathers dwell on baseball. On weekends, he teaches us French.

The cost is a certain confusion. At times I feel off-kilter, an alien at home plate. There is something out-of-sync in the swing of my baseball bat, something not quite kosher about my spoken English, a tendency to overarticulate, "public speak" it, which in the slirring slanguage of *Nooyawk* amounts to an accent.

It's the early Fifties, and the great cataclysm of World War II is still fresh in everyone's mind, so fresh nobody wants to be reminded. German is taboo, the tainted tongue of evil. Yet despite considerable pressure from relatives and peers, my parents refuse to blame the language. For to excise German would be to cut out their own tongue. The Jewish presence in Germanic lands dates back to Roman times. There is also the fact that my maternal grandmother, who lives with us, is hard of hearing and never learns English.

English is my best subject in school. I take pleasure in playing with words and ideas, constructing sentences, paragraphs, compositions, the way other kids like to build model cars and planes. English is the game I'm good at.

But the big abstractions like *Liebe* and *Tod* (Love and Death) resonate in familiar syllables. My grandmother gasps her last in the language of Goethe. And while I grow up and make my way in the world in English, I'm still all Hansel and Gretl at heart. Years later, in college, I find it difficult to get intimate in English. In a writing workshop, the instructor prods us to write and speak frankly and openly about sex. With my girlfriend of the moment seated beside me, I put my foot in my mouth. We're discussing the colorful language of one of Henry Miller's "Tropics," and I refer to the sexual organs as the stick and the hole, because my tongue is locked in a pre-adolescent limbo and, believe it or not, the English words penis and vagina are not a part of my vocabulary. I can still feel the sting of the All-American laughter.

A fellowship after college takes me to Germany, where I finally manage to align the foreign and the familiar. Things come together. *Liebe* and *Tod*, Love and Death mingle on the mattress and in the mind. I visit Dachau and do it in German. Returning to the States, I learn that love comes in many dialects. Fast forward to the time when I meet and marry my French wife (the pay-off for the pain of learning all those irregular verbs) and we decide to create a family of our own. . . .

There is no question in our minds but to raise our daughter bilingually, for she is a child of two cultures, two countries, two gates of perception. Though we live in New York, I force myself to speak French at home. (French is now my safe haven, my home plate, not the sharpened tool of my writer's trade nor the sticky tongue of childhood memory.)

French is our daughter's idiom of intimacy, English the language of her social contract. She is quick to correct my faulty Gallic puns and my wife's sometimes misaccented American. With a tongue and ear attuned to disparate sounds, she delights at age three in approximating Spanish on a vacation trip to Puerto Rico, and at four is already parrotting Italian in Rome. Our little family is a moveable border crossing.

Bilingualism also provides her with a psychological tool for self-regulation, a trick she taught herself. So, for instance, should she be at her wit's end in French, tired, frustrated and angry, she can shift tongue and identity. In English she can break out and save face.

Watching her easily perceive, process and express parallel realities, I value the hybrid seed my parents planted in me. Language is a revolving door. The realization that *the door* can also be *la porte* or *die Tür*, and that entry through it can lead to a simultaneous diversity of place, *the room*, *la chambre*, or *das Zimmer*, makes of the world a wonderland and of every child a virtual Alice.

Somewhere along the way, bilingualism got a bad name in the U.S. It became a catchword for the promulgation of bad English, as if to speak more than one language inevitably means to speak them badly. Need we be reminded that monolingualism is the exception, not the rule, worldwide? In most places, people speak two or more languages. Fortunately for my daughter, French still carries a certain cachet in the States and ruffles no xenophobic bristles.

We Americans come from around the globe. Dig a little and all the dialects of Babel come pouring out of the closet. Few families may be able to offer a built-in Berlitz along with the toilet training and table manners. But somewhere in the attic there's a bundle of letters scribbled in Italian, Spanish, Mandarin, Yiddish, Gaelic or Hindi. The next door neighbor's grandfather sings Scottish ballads, Navaho chants or Neapolitan love songs. Foremost among my family values is a sense of relativity, an ear for otherness, a developed taste for peppermint and chocolate and all the other flavors of the melting pot.

SHOWDOWN

Judy Blunt

Grounded to her room, my daughter shook out
wings on her way up the stairs, spread them
at the window, then bailed out of childhood
in freefall, an evolution of will I caught
by chance as she sailed off the eaves
to the back lawn, a flash of color
filling ten empty feet of air, and gone.
Captured two blocks from home, she weighs
my invitation and shrugs, folds herself, clipped
and calm into the car, surrendering
nothing on the short ride back, discovery
defined in lofts and curves pulled sharp
as sealing wax, solid as new muscle,
as final as that.

There will be no humble retreat
from this one, no return
of the martyred princess who drifted
through past trials with great show
and moderated sighs. At 16 she's grown

a first way to leave, and I find it
impossible to choose between fear and pride
at her poise, this defiant crossing
of lines that separate a mother
and a daughter, stepping into power
she's pieced together from scraps of mine.

Right now I can imagine
no ritual of distraction, no moving on
to other things with this near-woman
caged in my house, cocked and sure
on her feet, bangs spoiled stiff
over eyes that measure me
by inches, this
girl, pacing by the window, turning
to stare outside, leaning to touch
the pane with no reflection, no
backward glance and nothing
but time, spinning, loaded
on the tips of her fingers.

COMMON CLAY

Susan Vreeland

I smack the clay onto the wheelhead and begin to center when Mom calls to ask again about her new hearing aid, the second time this morning, the second time I have to wash my hands to pick up the phone. Other potters in the studio use it too.

"We have an appointment Thursday," I say. "I'm taking you. Look on your calendar. On the wall behind the phone. February 15. You see it written down?"

I wait while she sets down the phone.

"Oh, yes, here it is. Thursday. This Thursday?"

"This Thursday. In three days. Today's Monday. It's all arranged."

When she hangs up I start the wheel again. The clay whirls under my fingers, cool and rapturous, rising as if by magic. It's all over in a matter of minutes and I begin another. The phone rings. I have to wash my hands again. Kitaoji, the master potter in the co-op, is mixing glaze and I don't want to trouble him.

"You know my hearing aid is giving me trouble these days," she says.

"Mo-om. I just told you—"

"Oh." A pause. "I'm sorry I'm so dumb," she says and hangs up. The injury I've done her stings *me*, but in a quarter of an hour all she'll remember is a vague malaise.

Twenty minutes pass, a large ginger jar, wider shoulders and narrower base than I usually make, a greater risk. Kitaoji raises both eyebrows in approval as he passes by. For him, the epitome of subtlety, this is praise, and I am gladdened. I search for the essence of balance, the discovery of the moment when effort is no longer necessary and the clay lives, independent. The phone rings again. I'm at a critical moment, and have to true up the thin wall before I leave it, even for a few minutes. It's porcelain and may sink. "Let the answering machine take it," I say to him. "It's my mom." Her message is the same, and there's another, fifteen minutes later, more distracted, more intense. "I don't know what I'll do without my hearing aid."

I wonder if the effort of her calls wearies her, or if, because she forgets, there is no tiredness.

I used to visit her twice a week in that kindly-enough repository for the shrunken, the sick and baffled, until she looked at me with a strange curiosity once, wonder in her face tipped sideways. Now, despite the semi-annual show in our loft co-op only weeks away, I visit every other day, to insure the connection, forestall the inevitable.

Still, it sneaks up on me. One day when I arrive she points and says, "You have paint on your pants."

"No, it's glaze. Or clay maybe."

"Whatever for?"

"I make pots. I'm a potter. That's how I make my living."

"Imagine that. You mean bowls and cups?" she asks.

All my preparations for this are burned away in an instant. "Yes. Remember I brought you a vase once? Cobalt blue glaze?" I make the shape with my hands cupped over air, not that I think it will make her remember, but because doing so, carving space into line, is natural for my hands to do.

"Well, you must be very special," she says.

"And you are too. Do you know why?"

"No."

"Because you're my mother."

"I am?"

Only a soft chuckle escapes her, and I realize that chaos can be a quiet, gentle thing. I take her hand in mine, her hand that had braided my hair, had written funny notes in my lunch sacks, whacked me when I did wrong, and I stroke the fingers one by one from knuckle to nail. The curvature of the white moon following exactly the curvature of the yellowing tip sweeps me with a seasurge of the past. I don't know what is worse, Mom not knowing who I am and what I've done for her, or her not knowing what she's done for me, shaping me from babyhood. I know it *should* be the latter, for the sake of her peace. I know it *should* be.

The silkiness of clay soothes me, responds to my slightest pressure, its shape the visible record of the history of its influences. I'm working on teapots that are perfect rounds, that have perfect integrity, shoulder matching shoulder, the languid spout curving upward just so. I need to get it absolutely right. Over the next couple of days, to understand in my fingers the truth of the form, I make a dozen identical ones; only their spouts and handles will be different. In my mind's eye I try to see the shape of blackness held within, like a lung, or like the space where memory should reside, that shapely emptiness as solid as the clay itself. But the inner realm eludes me and my mind turns again to what Mom's present thoughts might really be.

The next week the ache of her not recognizing me is replaced with the ache of me not recognizing her. She is wearing a mint green sweat suit, just like the other patients. And tennis shoes. Tennis shoes! She's never worn them. Thought they looked like men's shoes. All the patients, I notice, have them now.

"When did you start wearing tennis shoes?" I ask.

She looks down curiously at her feet, lifts up her legs, heels together, toes outward, then wiggles them and shrugs. The answer, apparently, isn't important. I remember shopping with her at—, but why remember? "Yours are cleaner then the others," I say, reaching for a shred of identity. She laughs as if I made a joke.

Because *Where is everyone?* has become a refrain, I've brought some photos. I spread them out on the table and tell her the stories that match them.

"All these are the family. See, here's Jane and Jeremy.

"Oh yes, what ever happened to her?"

"She's in Alaska. She married a fellow who works on the pipeline."

It hurts me that she doesn't remember her own quilt, first place at the county fair, that photo showing her elated smile, the quilt, her original design, hanging behind her, the blue ribbon pinned to its edge. In another, the church choir stands behind her, the soloist, when she sang with perfect clarity, "There is a balm in Gilead to make the wounded whole."

"Mom, you were something special."

"I was?" She looks incredulous.

The effect of these events has dissolved. Losing a past seems to her at most, annoying, like losing a sock, an earring. No, a key.

She touches another photo with a cautious index finger. "Who is that man?" she asks, her curiosity apparently more powerful than any shame of not knowing.

"That's Papa. He was your husband."

Her eyes widen, she leans toward the image, scrutinizing its mystery, but she says nothing.

Neither can I.

I pack up the photos; there are some she didn't even look at. The one with the quilt I tape to her wall so the nurses will see, will know.

The shape is in my hands now and I can almost work without my mind engaged. On the second teapot of the morning some darkness pushes me and I stretch the form, distort it, make the shoulder over-broad as if to hold the weight of massive sorrow, a move that leaves more lateral unsupported clay at the rim than can usually hold itself intact. I twist the spout so it's unpourable, to reach for something uncommon, where function bows to sculpture and "teapot" itself is hardly recognizable. Even though I overwork the clay, it's strangely freeing.

For days we glaze and load the kiln. Kitaoji says a little prayer and lights some incense before he lights the big burners. Everyone in the co-op works restlessly and frets. The pots will bear evidence on their surfaces of the memory of fire. Those that survive will show that they faced the fire, have been tempered, tested, threatened with destruction yet have withstood the heat. Why one survives and the other perishes is a mystery.

Two days of cooling and we open the kiln. Kitaoji murmurs something in Japanese. I hold my breath. We caress them, our own and others', as we lift them out, still warm, each one showing the effects of all the minerals and gasses that have swirled close in the fiery air. It is a good firing. Only one is lost, my distorted teapot, caved in and sunken, its inner secret shape too widely gaping, too wild for the clay to bear, its thin shoulder surrendering to the weight of gravity.

"Sometimes the fire takes even the best, to keep us humble," Kitaoji says quietly.

I consider, for a moment, letting Mom see it before I toss it out. For all my thinking, I cannot find the effects in Mom of her having lost my sister at eight to scarlet fever, of her having sung solos for a decade, the congregation uplifted by her voice clear as a thrush at daybreak, and in that moment I feel the cold clamp of negative space. I lay it in the trash bin, and begin to miss her while she is still here, before she takes her leave.

I've brought her Toblerone chocolate and we eat it in the calming, celadon-colored common room.

"You know when we lived in Vienna, I always used to make you hot chocolate at night."

"No Mom. I never lived in Vienna. You did, but only as a child. It must have been your mother who made chocolate."

"She's coming for me, you know. We're going home."

"No Mom. This is your home. California. You've lived here forty years. I was born here. Remember how you got here? After the war? With Papa?"

Slowly she squints her eyes. Her cheeks lift to shape an eroded hilly landscape. I wonder, for the hundredth time, how it feels to rummage through shards of shifting memory.

"Please please please don't make me think it out." Her forehead reshapes itself and her eyes glisten wet like transparent glaze the moment before she buries her face in her hands. "I don't know where I'm supposed to be."

I go back to the loft and smash the teapots that are imbalanced, the imperfect seconds. The crashing sound is strangely satisfying. Kitaoji rushes inside from the kiln patio. His face is porcelain. Quickly I look from him to the rubble. "Well, you said that Hamada cut through his first 500 pots."

"That was when he was a beginner." His voice drops. "The show's three weeks away."

We run out of rutile and Kitaoji needs another load of clay. It's my fault. I should have ordered it, so I go with him in his rattly truck to our supplier across the city even though it's my visit day with Mom. I help him load his clay so the work goes quickly and I ask if he wouldn't mind stopping at the home on the way back. "I'll make it quick. You don't have to come in if you don't want to."

"Of course, I will," he says.

I introduce him—Kitaoji Yanagi. "I share his studio, Mom, and learn a lot from him."

He extends his hand, makes a slight bow.

"Are you from Japan?" A sudden worry shoots right through my chest.

"Yes, I was born in Shigaraki, but I am a citizen now."

"So is—, she," Mom says and points to me. "A citizen. Now. But she was born abroad. In Vienna."

I cast him a sideways look, untruth's discomfort gnawing.

"Oh yes. Yes, a country full of mountains. Like my own. My town is in the mountains, near the clay."

"Mine isn't, so much. But when she was a little girl we took her to the mountains. To, to Lech. It was a long way. She cried in a tunnel it was so dark and long."

"I never—"

A lovely soft shine glassing her eyes makes me bite back my conviction that it was condescending not to correct her, that it was the easy way out.

"Yes you did, and on the way back too. But you loved the wildflowers in the meadows, especially the cream colored ones that smelled like vanilla—what are they called? Stra—, Straph—" She shakes her hands at not remembering, but goes on. "And the air so clean and sharp inside your nose, and the cowbells echoing high and low, and the mountains, oh the mountains, they were like—" She raises her arms and looks up, uplifted by their soaring.

She doesn't finish, but the bravery with which she

launched the sentence trusting that she'd land some-where on solid ground warms me with pride.

"Don't you remember?" Urgency makes her shake her hands again and a tightness threatening her euphoria forms around her mouth.

"Each one a different shape," I say. "White as porcelain. Yes, Mom, they were magnificent."

For that instant, living in the moment with her is freeing, airy. Perhaps she is more centered than I am. The world may be spinning around her, mountains, people whirling in and out of rooms, but she is at its center, knowing those are her hands at the end of those arms, that that is her breath moving in and out of the dark center of her being.

Afraid that truth will suddenly crash and splinter, I say we have to go.

"I am honored to meet you," Kitaoji says, and my vision blurs.

As he opens the truck's door for me he says, "She is full of poetry."

Back at the studio I throw recklessly, the clay unwieldy on the wheelhead, but I lift anyway, too soon, with hardly an effort at centering, airily, with it wildly off, but I don't fight it as it rises wobbly, one side higher than the other. I feel as if my skill had vanished and I was a novice again, the clay uncontrollable, lurching with a life of its own.

I curve in its sides, bring in the lip and practically close it off, to make its dark interior shape unknown, leaving only a breath-wide opening. I cut the misshapen pot off the wheelhead, a vertical wavy egg, the marks left by my pressure oddly interesting and its struggles to be upright full of pathos.

Kitaoji stops in his unloading. "Beautiful," he says. "It has identity *and* mystery."

"Really?" I turn it to admire its lines. "If it survives the fire, should I exhibit it?"

He nods. "What will you call it?"

I look at it again. "History."

Part 4

A SENSE OF PLACE

HOUSE WITH CHILDREN

Richard Tillinghast

First the white cat named after Indians
Slipped in—too fat by half,
White marked with five black spots like sudden stones
In the snow—poked in through his hidden door,
Set flowing through the house a draft,
A chill tangled in the winter of his fur.

Alerted to those skulks, those leaps, those claws,
The sparkless energy-efficient
Furnace fired, pouring warmth through every vent
Of the house's two-storey stucco repose.

Julia slept her seven summers' worth
On a cloud of goose down, hugged by cushioned
    paws,
Dreaming. The wind blew out of the north.
Josh sprawled among paper fantasies.

Even Andrew rested from his wonderings,
His pages of lion, witch, and so forth.
Their three doors swayed in the warm domestic breeze
As Iroquois strolled past in his wanderings.

Drawn, was it, by the fragrance of marriage, he leapt
To the bed where the man woke and the woman slept
And the three-years' life between them burned fitfully
In a moment of fever, then woke laughing soundlessly.

Charles woke, and cooled his hands on the cat's chill fur.
In the clock's dimness white and dark spots blended.
The mercury stuck high, snow hung suspended
Like a V of geese over Canada.
The house and its people lodged secure
That night. Snow fell nowhere but Narnia.
There at the back of the wardrobe a door
Between the deep cold and the greatcoats stood ajar.

YOU CAN GO HOME AGAIN

Ellen Goodman

The car was packed to the roof with their luggage, their baby stroller, their diaper bag and all the other goodies sold as optional equipment with each new child. The husband had wrapped his son like a sausage into a swaddling of a snowsuit and put him, too, into the back seat.

The couple was headed home for the holidays. This time I was driving them to the airport, that first way-station on their annual migration. They carried with them the proof of belonging to the family on the other side of the air route: The husband bore his wedding band, the wife her freckles; the boy wore his red hair, which had been officially declared "exactly like" that of his grandfather.

Soon the wife's family would be together, all in the same area code. For once, no one would be directly dialed. For once they would be person to person . . . in person.

The roadway to the airport was already jammed. Day by day it was building to the peak load, the crescendo of traveling horrors, Thanksgiving Eve. That night the most penny-pinching soul damned the torpedoes and full-fared ahead. Home for the holidays.

It was good to be going home, the wife said to her husband as he struggled with the small boy trying to liberate his baby feet from the snuggy. He agreed.

He remembered something from one of the obituaries written last week about Margaret Mead. Being a citizen of the world, she said, meant being at home in many places. Holding his baby, he wondered about that. How many of us actually do feel at home in many places? How many more of us simply feel strange away from home?

The couple had spent their childhoods in other area codes—503 and 312—and in other environments. Each was a transplant, a cutting from a family tree, or at least a family plant. When they were young, everyone had simply expected that they would put down their roots wherever there was "the best opportunity." Now, sometimes, the wife remarked that the most transportable plant—the Wandering Jew—wasn't named for a willing immigrant but for a historic exile.

It wasn't the first time I had driven friends to the planes or trains or buses that took them away to their families. Many of my friends need a holiday to go home; many accept the idea that long distance is the next best thing to being there. And don't think much about what's best.

My family, on the other hand, has always been there. Through luck and choice, we share not only an area code but a zip code. Together we own eight bridge chairs, one thirty-cup percolator and a single electric drill. We play musical children and cars. Like some collective, with more enthusiasm than skill we trade: knitting lessons for disco lessons, nursing for gardening, carpentry for listening, day care for storytelling.

We complain to each other and about each other. We have helped each other sometimes and other times wrestled with our inability to help. We have been the keepers of our continuity. The people we can tell the truth about our children.

"Any marriage," W. H. Auden once wrote, "is infinitely more interesting and significant than any romance, however passionate." Well, I was never sure of that. But I have always thought that any family—with its history and its soap-opera intensity—was more interesting than any other collection of people.

So I suppose my own experience has made me question the notion that it is normal to leave home and vaguely suspect to stay. We are regarded as either "strong enough" to make it on our own or "not daring" enough to take the risk.

Our nation was founded by leavers; we are the grandchildren of leavers. We are a people who peculiarly regard self-fulfillment as an independent activity and who look upon our family lives as exercises in self-denial.

If we were playing a national game of word association, how many of us would identify the word "personal" with "growth," and "family" with "obligations"?

It seems that we continually jettison our support systems to avoid obligations and lose our context in the pursuit of a "better life."

"Each society," wrote Dr. Mead, "has taken a special emphasis and given it a full and integrated expression at the expense of other potentialities of the human race." We have taken the "I" over the "we"; potential over history.

My passengers were upwardly mobile, with emphasis on the mobile. They had left home for better schools in area code 415 and then for jobs in 202 and 212. Now they lived in 617 and had parents who touch-dialed their grandchildren. They were "at home" only on holidays. And wondered what they had gained and what they had lost.

But today, as the car finally pulled up to the entrance, the couple tumbled out grasping strollers and sausage, carrying with them an air of vacationers. They were people for whom family was not a routine but an occasional pleasure-seeking trip. So they went home excited. And I went home . . . thankful.

AURORA, JULY DOWNHILL

Pamela Gemin

Fresh from a rainstorm
I walk the hill down
from my first aunt Dorothy's,
down this narrow lane I know by heart,
bordered by purple milkweeds,
fern fronds, fool's oats,
pincherry trees,
and the buttercup wands we waved
under our cousins' chins.

Downhill, past my great aunt's house and garden,
cooler than October here
July's last night; chilly under muslin,
feet cold in summer sandals,
under them this road, the stony lumps of it
stuck in the tar like toads.

Downhill, past the *bobwire* fence
stretched open on the path to Carlsen's crick.
Fence of rusty metal thorns

(the better to *infect* you!),
of backs bent over sideways,
slashed ankles, bleeding palms.

And all for a brook trout
dipped in flour, real butter-fried:
to suffer the feel of the doomed
red worm on your hook;
that flash of fighting colors
when the fish bit,
silver belly puffing in and out;
the look in her eye you took with you;
the tickle of her thin bones
no cough could clear.

Down, past the maples
that shaded our horses;
down past the stream
still clear enough to read through;
down past the barn and haybed;

down past the jagged copper bluff
we climbed to scribble our true loves' names.

Down to the riverbank muck, straight down,
where toeprints must be fossilized somewhere,
The swipe of our muddy feet
as we ran up momentum, the push, the jump,
the sting of hair on eyelids,
the burn of the rope in our hands
as we swung out over the snake-black water,
screaming.

My Grandma Sara and all of her daughters,
all the O'Riley Girls,
lugged gallons of hand-filled ravioli
under these willows, and racks of homemade pastries,
hundred-pound honey-glazed hams,
dozens of French Canadian pork pies,
tins and tins of bars, bars — butterscotch,
coconut, chocolate chip, cherry-cheese,
apricot, oatmeal, nutmeg —
then they said we all should *have some more* . . .

Those days the men played cards
on picnic tables, smoking,
barechested, lean-muscled, young,

unshaven on their day off,
children on their laps
and happy with beer.

Before my cousin Kenny
        drowned in the lake,
before my cousin Nicky
        died of meningitis,
before my Grandpas' hearts gave out
        or Uncle Frank drove into that wall,
before cancer moved into Aunt Rose
and Aunt Rose moved out,
        or I lost my Grandma Sara
        (first to the t.v. preachers,
        then again
        when her kidneys quit).
Before Lee Ann's divorce,
        and Maggie's, and Little Sara's,
before Uncle Benny's strokes,
        when they still said he drank
        on account of The War,
before any of us knew
        those secrets
        we dug so relentlessly for
        would rush up from the caverns
        to scald us blind,

this is the place we lay in dozens,
cool-skinned and damp-haired,
fresh from the river,
dozing together, hard little bellies full,
in perfect safety.

Now thirty years gone,
as simply and much
as sun and rain, I'm still welcome
all down this hill.
And everything around me bows deeply,
steps aside,
to make room.

A PUERTO RICAN STEW

Esmeralda Santiago

I'm in my kitchen, browsing through Puerto Rican cookbooks, when it hits me. These books are in English, written for people who don't know a *sofrito* from a *sombrero*. Then I remember the afternoon I returned to Puerto Rico for the summer after 15 years of living in the United States. The family gathered for dinner in my mother's house. The men settled in a corner of the living room, while Mami and my sisters chopped, washed, seasoned. I stood on the other side of the kitchen island, enjoying their Dance of the Stove with Pots and Pans—the flat metal sounds, the thud of the refrigerator door opening and closing, the swish of running water—a percussive accompaniment enhancing the fragrant sizzle of garlic and onions in hot oil.

"Do you cook Puerto Rican?" Norma asked as she cored a red pepper.

"No," I answered, "I never got the hang of it."

"How can you be Puerto Rican without your rice and beans?" joked Alicia.

"Easy," said Mami. "She's no longer Puerto Rican."

If she had stabbed me with the chicken-gutting knife in her hand it would have hurt less. I swallowed the pain. 'Si, Mami," I said, "I have become *Americana*."

"I knew it the minute you stepped off the plane."

I parried with "Wasn't that what you wanted when you first brought us to New York?"

As Mami split the chicken, her voice rose, indignant: "I only wanted the best for you."

The dance was over, a knife suspended above tomato halves, rinse water running through rice clear as sunshine. I walked away, pushed by their silence—my mother, my sisters, my brothers-in-law. No one followed me, or challenged her assessment of me as a turncoat who had abandoned her culture. I stood in the gravelly yard, the soles of my sandals separating me from the ground as if I were on stilts, unable to touch my native soil, unable to feel a connection. I wanted to cry, but would not give them nor myself the satisfaction of tears. Instead, I leaned against a fence and wondered if her words hurt so much because they were true.

Whatever I was, Puerto Rican or not, had been orchestrated by Mami. When I was 13, she moved us from rural Puerto Rico to Brooklyn. We were to learn English, to graduate from high school, to find jobs in clean offices, not factories. We were to assimilate into American society, to put an end to the poverty she was forced to endure for lack of an education.

I, the oldest, took up the challenge. I learned English so well that people told me I didn't "speak like a Puerto Rican." I gave up the bright, form-fitting clothes of my friends and relatives for drab, loose garments that would not brand me as a "hot tomato." I developed a formal, evasive manner when asked about my background. I would not admit to being poor, to living with my mother and 10 sisters and brothers in a three-room apartment. I would tremble with shame if newspapers identified a criminal as Puerto Rican.

Mami beamed when I got a job as a typist in Manhattan. She reminded me that I was to show my sisters and brothers the path to success without becoming "Americanized," a status that was never clearly defined but to be avoided at all costs.

That afternoon in her kitchen was the first time we had spoken in seven years. The grudge we held was so deep, neither could bridge it without losing *dignidad*, an imperative of Puerto Rican self-esteem. The break had come when I stopped being a "good" Puerto Rican girl and behaved like an American one.

At 21, I assumed I was old enough to live my life as I pleased. And what I pleased was a man a year older than Mami. I ran away with him, leaving a letter telling Mami I wouldn't be home after work because I was eloping. "Don't worry," I signed off, "I still love you."

She tracked me down to an apartment in Fort Lauderdale more luxurious than any we'd ever lived in, to say that if I returned home all would be forgiven. I refused. During those seven years, the man for whom I'd left my mother turned out to be as old-fashioned, possessive and domineering as she had seemed. From him, too, I ran away.

To question my Puerto Rican identity that afternoon in her kitchen was Mami's perfect comeback to what had surely been seven years of worry. It was also her way of recognizing her own folly. She had expected me to thrive in American culture, but I was to remain 100 percent Puerto Rican.

Mami came to realize the impossibility of such a demand, how difficult it is for someone from a "traditional" culture to achieve success in the United States without becoming something other than the person she set out to be. My one act of rebellion forced her to face what she had never expected. In the United States, her children would challenge her authority based on different rules of conduct. Within a year of my leaving home, she packed up the family and returned to Puerto Rico, where, she hoped, her children would be what they couldn't be in the United States: real Puerto Ricans.

I stayed behind, immersed in the American culture she feared. But I never considered myself any less Puerto Rican. I was born there, spoke its language, identified with its culture. But to Puerto Ricans on the island during my summer there, I was a different creature altogether. Employers complained that I was too assertive, men said I was too feminist, my cousin suggested I had no manners, and everyone accused me of being too independent. Those, I was made to understand, were Americanisms.

Back in the United States, I was constantly asked where I was from, and the comments about my not looking, behaving or talking like a Puerto Rican followed me into the era of political correctness, when it's no longer polite to say things like that.

I've learned to insist on my peculiar brand of Puerto Rican identity. One not bound by geographical, linguistic or behavioral boundaries, but rather, by a deep identification with a place, a people and a culture which, in spite of appearances, define my behavior and determine the rhythms of my days. An identity in which I've forgiven myself for having to look up a recipe for *arroz con pollo* in a Puerto Rican cookbook meant for people who don't know a *sombrero* from a *sofrito*.

HELMETS

Pete Fromm

As our buses rushed into the desert I sat alone in my seat, nearly lulled to sleep by the endless flitting of the sagebrush and the mingling conversations of the other engineers. The sun had just begun to rise at our backs when suddenly, apparently out of nowhere, the Helmet family appeared.

I didn't sit up any straighter at first—a car, after all, while rare this far out, is not unheard of. But as it passed, going the opposite direction, toward town, I caught a glimpse inside. And what I saw was a family: father behind the wheel, mother at the other door, son and daughter occupying the rear seat. Tediously normal, if it were not for the fact that everyone in this family wore helmets. Not steel military issue, but flashy white things. Most likely, nothing more substantial than bicycle helmets. I did sit up straighter then, turning to stare, though, by then, the car was already long gone.

For a moment, I simply gazed at the empty road. Then I glanced around the bus for someone I might tell about what I'd seen. But, with my coworkers an entire generation younger than myself, I rarely spoke on those long rides. So I settled back into my seat, making a mental note to tell Nancy about this strange family that evening during dinner. What in the world did they think they could protect themselves from?

After arriving at the facility, a small crisis in the magnetic containment project kept our team in meetings most of the day. I sat quietly through all of them, wishing I'd been left to work alone at my computer, never being quick enough to think of much to add to these lightning brainstormings. There was a great worry over the possibility of unwanted detonations, but, since my earliest days with DOE, we'd had a nearly unblemished safety record and I wasn't able to muster the same concern as the young men around me. These things always worked out. Instead of listening, I found myself wondering about that family and their helmets, nearly smiling as I imagined how an unwanted detonation would certainly ruin their safe day.

When the meetings finally wrapped up, the team broke into its usual groups, leaving me to get back to my workstation. I'd just flipped on my monitor when my supervisor, Mr. Becker, a thick-haired man half my age, blocked the exit to my cubicle. He smiled and asked if I'd had a chance over the weekend to consider our talk about early retirement.

Glancing at the monitor's cool blue, I slipped my hands beneath my legs. "Nancy and I discussed it, of course," I began, but I couldn't think of another word. Picking at the sturdy weave of the upholstery beneath my fingers, I started over. "Perhaps after ironing out some of this magnetic containment . . ."

But Mr. Becker interrupted, assuring me my work had been invaluable, but adding, with a small laugh, that he thought they'd be able to muddle on—although, of course I'd be sorely missed.

With a light slap on my shoulder, a habit of his I could barely stand, he asked me again to give it some serious thought. Before I knew it we were all hustling out of the buses for our sixty-mile ride back to civilization.

I picked at my dinner that night, Nancy waiting patiently to hear what was bothering me. She knows I'm not allowed to discuss my projects and, at times, that has been more helpful than I'd care to admit. But tonight she kept waiting, and finally, setting my silverware aside, I said, "Do you remember, Nancy, how exciting everything was when I first started?" Naturally, I'd been thinking a lot about those early days, when even the hush-hush nature of the work seemed to add a flair my life had never known.

"Of course," Nancy said, smiling. "Phyllis threw us the bon voyage party. As if Idaho were in another country."

"Public Relations has replaced the boundary signs again," I said. "INEL this time. Idaho National Engineering Laboratory."

Nancy's smile began to falter, but I continued. "Much less threatening than the Department of Energy Test Site, I suppose. But they've left up the military's 'No Trespassing' signs, and the 'Unexploded Ordnance Area' notices. Who do you suppose they think they're fooling?"

Nancy didn't answer, and I said, "Do you remember when Congress gave us all the money we could ask for? When people still thought we were doing something essential? When it wasn't something to try to hide, to be embarrassed about?"

I realized I'd raised my voice, but Nancy's eyes met mine.

"Those were the exciting years," she agreed, "when everything was so dangerous." But then, lowering her voice to a whisper, she added. "We made a world so dangerous we wouldn't even risk bringing children into it."

When I didn't answer, Nancy quietly raised her plate, asking for more.

"I don't know what's the matter with this country anymore," I muttered, but I forked a thin slice of ham onto Nancy's plate.

It wasn't until I saw the same family the very next day, again helmeted against the world, that I realized I'd forgotten to tell Nancy about them. I reminded myself all day long and, that evening, as soon as we were settled in for dinner, I said to Nancy, "I've seen the oddest thing the past two mornings."

Nancy raised an eyebrow.

I filled her plate and passed it to her. "A family," continued, "in a car. Coming to town as I go to work." ·

She listened quietly, a smile waiting to start at the corners of her mouth.

"Every one of them——" I said, pausing, letting the suspense build as I served myself, "mother, father, son, daughter—every one wears a helmet. Every day."

"Helmets?" Nancy asked, her smile breaking across her face, sure she was being teased.

"Helmets!"

"What in heavens for?"

I shrugged hugely. "They must believe it offers them some sort of extra protection. Something the rest of us don't have." My eyes widened in disbelief, accenting the mockery in my voice.

"You can't be serious, Wilton."

"I am, though," I said, smiling myself as I picked up my fork. "Can you believe the naiveté of some people? Why, with even our oldest projects, we could leave nothing of them but white shadows on the road! Helmets!"

Nancy looked at me then, her fingers picking at an ironed wrinkle on the tablecloth, her mouth for a moment as tight as the line in the material. She dipped her head to her dinner and when she looked back up she said they'd started a new program at the grade school where she volunteered. "The MAN project," she said it was called. "Men Are Nice. Some of those children have never known a man who's done anything but abuse them or their mother." She looked at me, shaking her head. "We're looking for men to read stories to them after school. Men just to be kind."

I nodded, but the change of subject wasn't lost on me. Nancy has never liked me talking about my work.

The family was there again the next morning, and the next, so regularly I ceased to be surprised by their appearance. In fact, I sat in my seat in the INEL bus and waited for them, tense until their little white sedan rolled past, their helmets flashing white inside. Only then did I ease back into my seat to begin pondering the day's tasks.

This went on for an entire week before I realized the family had begun to interrupt my thoughts even while I worked. I would find myself suddenly woken as if from a trance, staring into some unfinished design on my monitor, realizing I had only been wondering about that family and their silly helmets. Often I would have no idea how much time had been lost.

While perhaps I was never the department's most brilliant design engineer, I was always steady and I was frightened to find myself so easily distracted. The collapse of the cold war undoubtedly sapped some urgency, but even last month, though deeply shaken after first being interrogated about my interest in early retirement, an interest which is absolutely nonexistent, I was back on task within minutes.

The following morning, I listened to the young engineers discuss the newest round of layoffs until I saw the car rolling carefully toward us. As it hugged the shoulder, anticipating our line of buses streaking by, my mind suddenly filled with all the things we could do to their car and their preposterous notions of safety. The stark white outlines left by a nuclear flash weren't even necessary. We had the technology now to blow them into the air first, then atomize them, leaving not a trace of their vain hopes.

As soon as the car swooshed by, however, these thoughts left me quite shaken. I rarely allow myself to dwell upon the use of our work, particularly not in any way so personal or inappropriate. I decided I would have to track down the Helmet family, as Nancy had begun to call them, to see exactly what it was that they thought they could keep so safe.

The very next morning, I purposely missed my bus. Feigning annoyance for Nancy's sake, I scrambled into our car and raced out for the desert, hoping to find a spot to wait until I could follow the Helmet family to wherever it was they went. For the first time ever, I fabricated an excuse to explain my absence from work.

I'd just gotten turned around when the white sedan came over the hill, right on schedule, moving completely into the other lane as they went around me, as if I might fling open my door and step blindly into their path—completely unaware of the concept of safety. I pulled out and followed them into Idaho Falls.

The trailing was more difficult in town with the stoplights and traffic. My heart was pounding from a wild acceleration through a mostly yellow light when the white sedan first pulled over. They were in front of a school and I had to stop in the bus area. I watched as the daughter, probably no more than ten or eleven years old, hopped briskly out and started for the playground, already crowding with children.

She glanced over her shoulder, a slim, pretty, breakable child, long, black hair flowing from beneath her helmet. Following her glance, I saw her parents' car pulling back into traffic, but I hesitated. The girl was already working on the helmet's chin strap, peeling the helmet from her head and running her fingers through her hair to remove its crushing outline. She hid the helmet in her backpack and swung through the gateway bars of the playground, where she disappeared in a group of laughing girls.

The blare of the bus horn startled me so greatly I jerked forward without checking traffic, causing another, smaller, horn blast. A mother glared, the seats of her car filled with wide-eyed children. At the first available corner, I signalled and turned away, fleeing, having lost the white sedan during my study of their daughter—their daughter who didn't share their hopeless ideas of safety a second longer than necessary for appearances.

After driving pointlessly for several minutes, I headed back for the school. I wanted again to see that young girl, so like all the others, so childish looking, but already able to see with a clarity greater than her parents'.

But at the school the playground was empty, the children all safely inside, even the crossing guards heading for their cars, not to return until the lunchtime recess.

I didn't go to work that day, though I would have been little more than an hour late. For a long time I simply circled through town, hoping somehow that I might bump into the white sedan.

I considered going home, spending the day with Nancy, but I pictured sitting on the edge of the bed while she dressed for her afternoon at the school, clipping her earrings on, only half listening to the excuse I'd invented to explain being home in the middle of the day. Once she was gone, I'd walk through our house, my footsteps ringing off the hardwood floors, wondering for the first time how she filled all the hours.

It was nearly dark before I stopped my car in our driveway and spent the dinner hour telling Nancy what I'd accomplished at work that day.

The following morning, I again walked around the corner as if going to work. After waiting an appropriate time I returned home for the car keys, grumbling about missing the bus.

But this morning Nancy followed me out to the driveway. "Wilton?" she said, leaving it there for me to explain.

"What?" I asked, irritated by being forced to play simple.

"I don't remember you ever missing the bus before." She looked at me carefully, truly concerned. "Is everything all right? Everything at work?"

Ever since Mr. Becker had gone past the suggestion stage, I'd tried to come up with some way to tell Nancy about what they were still calling *early* retirement, though *forced* seemed considerably more accurate. But, after so long a time believing in my work, I didn't know what to say. I smiled at Nancy and shook my head. "Old-timer's disease," I said.

She smiled obediently, but it did little to dispel her worried expression. "You'd tell me, wouldn't you, Wilton? If there was something?"

I said, "Of course I would, Nancy."

She watched me back down the drive and, even after I turned the corner, I could feel her watching.

Worrying that people as careful as the Helmet family would surely recognize the same car following them in from the desert, I decided to wait for them at the daughter's school. My timing was off, perhaps due to my excitement, or my rush to get away from Nancy's questions, and I spent nearly half an hour parked in front of the school before the white sedan appeared.

I watched the girl repeat her movements of yesterday, as far as the unstrapping of the helmet, before I had to leave in order to follow the rest of her family. As I chased them across town, I wondered if the parents were at all aware of their daughter's duplicity. Or perhaps she was allowed to remove her helmet in school. Perhaps her parents were so adept at self-deception that they could imagine school as a safe haven, despite the contents of the nightly newscasts.

The car stopped at another school and even as I pulled in, several slots behind them, I wondered why the children attended different schools, schools so far apart. I had not yet had time to take in my surroundings.

Rather than the son simply leaping from the car as their daughter had, both front doors swung open. I nearly smiled at the recklessness of the move, the helmeted father actually stepping into the traffic lane. They met at the son's door and opened it for him. Then, together, they helped him toward the school door, his steps herky-jerky, decisionless, his head rolling this way and that, sometimes lolling as if its weight were simply too much for the thin neck.

Realizing what I was seeing, I averted my gaze, wiping at my forehead's sudden sheen of sweat, feeling little more than a Peeping Tom. Instead, I looked into the playground, awash with adults, more of them, it seemed, than children. Nearly all the children wore helmets, some much more severe than the son's white model, some heavy and leatherish, some even with faceguards, though the children never seemed out of catching range of an attendant, should their labored steps disintegrate into complete collapse.

At the door, as the parents stooped to kiss and pet him, I saw the unmistakable cast of the son's face, the features of whatever it is that causes all that.

The family disappeared inside for just a moment, then the parents reappeared alone, trotting to their car, hands fiddling with their chin straps. At the car, they flipped their helmets into the still-open door of the back seat. The father grazed a finger along his wife's shoulders as he moved around her on his way to the driver's seat and, though I'd planned to follow them, to see where they went next, I knew it was no longer necessary. I stayed where I was for quite some time, trying not to look into that awful playground, the white flash of the son's helmet unmistakable in the mass of globed heads.

I sat with my head down and my eyes closed until I'd regained some composure—an old trick of Nancy's—and then I eased into the street, wondering where to go. The quick tire screech was all the warning I had before the jolt and the sound of the metal.

The woman was flustered, but kind, more concerned with her helmeted daughter than any minor damage to her station wagon. I tried to give cash, but she laughed, saying a swap of insurance papers would be plenty. She seemed surprised not to know me, and was immediately standoffish when I said I wasn't here with a child. I followed her glance to the playground, where the attendants were trying to keep their flock from stumbling toward the excitement of our accident. I wondered for a horrified moment if there were people who actually came to gawk at these children and, without planning to, I said, "I'm new here. I'm still just checking into schools for our child."

I accompanied her all the way up the steps with her girl as she assured me that I could do no better than this school. The parents, too, were wonderful. And the support groups, if we were interested in that sort of thing. I said that indeed we were, my wife and I, and we formally introduced ourselves before returning to our cars, where I apologized once more.

I made it several blocks before pulling over and again lowering my head and closing my eyes.

I don't know how she managed it, if she'd been waiting by the window since I left or not, but Nancy was on the front step before I'd finished pulling into the driveway. Coming home in the middle of the morning, with the fender buckled, I knew there would have to be some explanation, but I'd been unable to collect my thoughts even toward a starting point.

Nancy met me at the car door, nearly blocking me in.

"Good morning," I said, sliding out and stepping around her toward the house. She was already dressed for her volunteer work with those children who'd never met a nice man.

"Wilton?" she said, following. "What is it, Wilton?"

I was sweating and my hand trembled as I reached for the doorknob.

"What happened to the car, Wilton? Have you been hurt?"

At the edge of the dining-room table, I glanced around our modest house and then turned and looked at Nancy, my wife of thirty-seven years. "They're forcing me to retire," I said, out with it all at once.

Nancy stared. "But the car? Are you all right?"

I waved that away. "Retired," I repeated. "I'm going to lose my work."

"I know how much your work means to you, Wilton," she said quietly. "But that doesn't explain this. What's happened?"

"I've been following the Helmet family," I said, surprising myself. "The helmets. They're not for what we thought. That family knows more about safety than we ever will." Suddenly I needed to sit down. "My work, Nancy. It's all I've ever had."

"What about the Helmet family?" she asked, pulling up one of the dining-room chairs and sitting beside me.

Briefly, I told her what I'd seen, how they wore the helmets only so their boy wouldn't be alone. I even told about the women who'd hit our car. "I had to lie to her," I said. "She thought I was just there to stare at those children."

"What did you tell her?" she whispered.

"I told her we had our own child. That I was simply looking for a place where he'd be welcome."

As I spoke, Nancy broke down and I held her and rocked her in those hard dining-room chairs, my head down over hers, my eyes closed tight.

MAMA'S ROOM

Nan Saville

I can sit back here
and hear you tell the stories,
though you've been gone for years,
your warmth shines in the eyes
of everyone who would smile at me.
Talking about the levee
and the rising water
that moved it back,
erasing the clover fields
and making skin and bone of that old cow
who ate the doll clothes
hung so carefully on the line to dry.
Telling how 'Naughton's body was crippled,
but his spirit soared to heaven and back
'cept for that one last time.
How his uncle, Buddy Crawford,
was a fine man, and it broke
his mama's heart because
he didn't deserve to die like that,

but he walked nearly a mile
with bullets meant for
some other colored fellow
in his chest
just in sight of her porch
where his legs could no longer
follow his will.
That year the mirrors wore black
and only darkness
was allowed in the house.
I can feel you look out at the world
through my eyes now;
So much of it is different
and much the same.
And the evening sun
stretches its fingers through the curtains
and colors patterns on the pale walls
and the moist summer air
wraps around me like your hug.

Part 5

•

WORK AND FAMILY

THE WOMAN WHO NEVER SLEEPS

Kevin Elliot Milam

It happened gradually. It was no
thin bid for fame, as the paper
claims. After years of six hours
a night not being enough, and still
nothing being done, I thought I'd stay
up an hour more—just to pay bills
on time for once. The next night
it was something equally innocuous
but necessary. Cleaning the kitchen,
washing dishes, I don't know. I didn't
think I was doing anything earth shattering
as night by night the minutes peeled off
from sleep. Then there were the five full
baskets of laundry, piled on the counter
so the baby wouldn't help—or the cats.
I remember that night, because just as I
finished, the alarm clock upstairs rang
and my husband meandered downstairs
as I marched the tower of folded laundry
upstairs. That day, it seemed silly
to lie down for an hour before the baby

cried and called for me at six. I had
time for everything after that. Already
I had begun to lie: "I nap when the baby
does," I told my husband. "I don't need
much sleep any more." The older children
were less easily tricked, since they saw
me most nights, when bad dreams woke them.
After a few weeks (as best as I could
figure—what are weeks in days that do not
end?) all the obvious things had been done.
Now I called forth my more esoteric skills
and learned to weave rainhats from discarded
plastic bags. I planted all the seeds
we had saved for next year. I began to plan
painting the house by moonlight, vacuuming
the garage rafters, building fences to hide me
from the neighbors. At night I rattle
through the bedrooms as my family sleeps.
I photograph their flat dream worlds.
They do not feel me skimming by.

NIGHTS MY FATHER

Donna Masini

We never knew exactly what our father did
in dark basements, late into the night.
His work clothes, cellar smells.
The dark came out of him.
Dirt green, creased black,
ACE in big red letters
a yellow diamond stitched across his back,
below the earth with rats and tar,
roaches, spiders, waterbugs.
Only he knew the way out.

Underground by the oilburners
where the heat went dead
he crawled into iron mouths
hauled out fists of oily sludge.
Could a man get trapped in there?
Scars, creases where grease seeped in, never came out,
thick soot worms under his nails,
he rolled the hose from tanks to valves

ladies, alligators curled in basements.
When the harbor froze he slept on the floor by his truck.

In the middle of the night there was something
in our kitchen,
rattling through the silverware
in our kitchen drawer.
In the gold night light, a bear,
the thick fur breathing.
I aimed a gun. I shot.
The fur parted.
It was my father. His good suit pressed
but the hands stuck out: greasy hands,
so black the creases darkened as he washed them.

He didn't need anyone. He could do it alone.
Boilers humming, clanging, air banging, heat building.
There she goes, he'd yell,
at the center of the earth,

where the heat is, and rough hands,
men's hands. They way they touch.
Warm men with rough hands
cha-cha bossa nova
the snoring comes from that place,
low sounds the body makes.

Our father heated people in winter,
and he danced our mother
with the grace of a bear,
under red bulbs,
by the Christmas tree
the pudding black, so black,
a cake of shaking oil.

I remember him in winter
mornings when I wake,
the bridge hanging across the street in the snow

trucks skidding, whispering in the icy sun.
The whispers from the bedroom,
the creaking of the floor, the whispers,
the dark something dropping,
then he snorted through the night
water dripped, radiators popped.

Don't touch him, we screamed,
as he came through the door,
my head in his work clothes.
The dark coming out.
All night the glazy stare at the TV set.
Heart. Get it going. He begins to stamp and steam.
He went under, down under streets, gratings,
the places men went.
Could a man get trapped in there?
Graves. Caves. Boilers. Crawling.
Nights I heard him humming.

JOBS

Al Maginnes

Tools had secrets
to make work get done:
claw hammer, power saw
I never had the skill to use.
My hands blistered to fit
shovel, rake, and hoe handles.
When I got a carpenter's bench
for my eighth birthday, it was my father
who built a bookcase, bird houses,
a wooden key with hooks to hang real keys on.
I watched, trying to discover
the life hidden inside tools.
He tucked his lower lip under his teeth,
hammered and measured his way
inside some concentration
I could not enter, my first glimpse
of the work men invent to answer
a bidding buried in the clank
and gearwork of the daily shuffle.
It would be a few years
before I walked onto a construction job
and learned men were identified

by the jobs they were paid for.
At the finish, they left their names
on I-beams, staircases, and backs of panels.
It was there my hands hardened
with the work underneath them,
and I learned the rhythm that progresses
toward the long breath at the day's end.
I scratched my name
in the wet concrete of a grade beam.
In my first office job, the progress
of paper was endless. I signed nothing
to mark the work of my softening hands.
I wanted to build something
in my unpaid hours that would hold
solid and symmetrical as a right angle,
my name the only inessential thing.
My father never signed his bird houses,
but I have seen his name scribbled
over and over in the frantic work
of a young bird's wings
as it apprentices itself
to the job of flight.

GRANMA'S APRON

Mary Helen Ponce

In memory of Granma Pepita (Josefina Altamirano),
who in the 1930s picked cotton in the San Joaquin Valley

The funeral is over; the guests fed on pan dulce and chocolate say goodbye. Tired of sitting still, the children run freely in the noonday sun. Inside granma's old house mother rinses the cups and dishes given free with Rinso soap. They were granma's pride and joy. She straightens the velvet cushions sent from Korea with love. Anxious to leave, I pace the worn linoleum, peek out the window, surprised to see robins nesting in granma's trees.

Long before granma began to die, her garden started to wither. One cold winter, the apple tree, planted when I was a boy, shivered, then split in two. In a sudden windstorm, the walnut tree nurtured by granma, held up by boards that from afar resemble crutches, groaned, then stooped over, never to rise again. Yet steadfast geraniums, cuttings from neighbors and friends, blistering red with glossy green leaves creep along the old picket fence.

Mother calls me indoors to sift through dusty boxes. High school yearbooks in tissue paper secured with twine brought home from the work fields, football programs yellowed with time, postcards from Korea. My fingers brush a crocheted doily, manteles of bleached flour sacks, a baby blanket smelling of mothballs, and come to rest on thick dark canvas.

"This was your granma's," mother tells me, as she rubs her tear-stained cheek against a faded apron. "She wore it when she picked cotton. ¿Te acuerdas?"

Memory floods my tired mind: Granma in the cotton fields of Shafter, McFarland, Delano. Granma straining beneath the cotton sack to which, between dusty rows, I hung on for dear life. Granma sharing tacos of fried potatoes, weenies, carne asada, rolled at five in the morning while I still slept, food washed down with coffee kept in an empty jam jar. Granma sitting upright in her rocking chair, worn Bible in hand, thanking her God for a job well done.

"She was over fifty," mother reminds me, "pero se fue al fil. I was en el Keene with TB; the social worker tried to take you from her. We were poor, m'hijo, so alone." From far off mother's voice drifts past me like dust swirls along a country road.

"Yo puedo trabajar," she told the craggy foreman who looked her up and down, then snickered loudly. "She strapped the cotton sack around her shoulders, plunked you at the very edge, staked a row for herself. All summer long she worked with you at her side."

The apron feels heavy in my hands, its sulphur smell clogs my every pore. Granma, of peasant stock, short and wide, her strong arms covered with dust. Granma in the sweltering July heat sipping water from a dented canteen. Granma in a faded dress, thick frame hoisting high the sack that slithered up and down the dusty field.

Granma's calloused hands that reeked of mentholatum, wrapped each night with clean white rags. Blistered hands that held me tight.

I cradle the apron in my smooth hands, empty the side pocket of lint, looking for pieces of granma. I see granma at the kitchen table, her wide feet resting on the worn linoleum. The tin sewing basket stands next to the kerosene lamp that sheds its steady light. Spools of colored thread, assorted pins and needles, the round pincushion stitched from scraps. The apron, sewn late at night, was cut from old work pants, stitched after she first mended shirts, torn jeans and worn socks. As she sewed, granma hummed church hymns sung at the Apostolic church. Spanish words of faith, compliance, perseverance. In the dim sunlight I touch the sturdy material, poke with my finger the wide buttonholes, feel the double-stitched seams that held our home together.

I say goodbye, hold tight mother's thin frame, make vague promises of visits to come. I hold the faded apron, smooth down the creases made by time, roll it tight in Sunday's news, then slowly drive past cotton fields of childhood, granma's apron by my side.

FOUND MONEY

Patti Tana

Almost every day I find
a penny on the street.
And if the penny faces up
I call it luck.
And if it's down
I call it money.

When I was young
I helped my mom clean a store at night
after her regular job.
I'd spray counters with ammonia
that went up my nose and stung my eyes
then rub away the fingerprints
with a soft cloth.
I'd scrape gum from the floors
and hold the pan as she swept
in the dust and black dirt.

Sometimes I'd find coins in the dressing room.
I even found a dollar

behind a row of gowns.
No matter if I found a dollar or a dime
Mom made me leave it with a note
on the big wooden register.

Once I found a wallet
on the floor of a movie theater.
No name. No pictures. Only money.
Even in the dark I could see
it was red, smooth plastic red.
I looked at my mother
and she looked away.

Almost every day I find
a penny on the street.
And if the penny faces up
I call it luck,
And if it's down
I call it money.

THE OLDER FATHER

Jean Rysstad

What did I know then? What does any child know at ten or twelve? I knew from bits and pieces of conversations between my parents, who never dwelt on a problem, that my father was not well. If it was talked about at all, his heart condition was understated.

My parents had a general store in the village of Kintail on Lake Huron, Bluewater Highway #21. Our house was next to the store, a passageway the width of a strong, healthy man between the two. It was a brick store, yellow, this new business built from bricks of the inn my grandparents had when travellers on horse and buggy needed a stopping point between towns.

I call myself young. Thirty-eight in the fall. But I was the baby of our family and, in some ways, I still feel the baby trying to understand my part and place in things. Listening and watching.

My father would be 94 if he were alive. Born in 1901, a year behind the year, he said, when anyone asked his age. Forty-eight when I was born. The early pictures of him with my sisters and brother show a stocky man, with straw-coloured curly hair, a chest thrown for posterity, for the photographers' pleasure, his own pleasure evident. There is that strong sense of a physical man, a strong physique. And the wit in the eyes and lips, as if after the picture is taken he has some comment to deliver, well-timed, apt.

One sister, who is perhaps the most like him, tells me he used to chase her around the house when she sassed him. He certainly never chased me. I had a different father. The older father.

I did not see anything unusual in our family situation. I thought I was lucky. I would not have traded Kintail for anywhere else that I knew or dreamed or read of. I considered us rich. Rich with interesting things to do as well as rich with things I could have access to without much effort. I was expected to work in the store as soon as I could add up a row of figures properly and write out a bill. First name, date, items, cost and total. The bill poked on a spike pounded in a slab of wood upended.

After school, the first thing I did was choose a treat. My "official" treat. I would have several more plus a bottle of pop later, when keeping store alone while my parents ate supper. I would eat and read in the post office part, spreading the paper out on the tilt-top desk where the stamps and money orders were kept. I listened for cars at the gas pumps. Neighbours got their own gas. Strangers honked the horn.

I would fill up the pop case, going to the basement for the stock. Wooden crates of Kist, Vernor's, Root Beer. Make the selection and carry the cases up the back stairs. Arrange them in the cooler, warm to the front of the display case, cool to the back, easiest reached.

Dad's tires were all piled in sizes in the basement of the store. Firestone, 650-15s, and bring my specs Jean,

he'd say when the phone rang and he needed to use the fine print tire catalogue to quote a price. He sold new and fixed old. There was a reservoir of rainwater in the basement and a bare light bulb dangling above it. Sometimes, when I came home from school, Dad would be in the basement repairing a tire, holding a tube under the water, under the light, watching for the leak, the bubbles. I would put my finger on the spot while he got a rag, dried the tube, cut a patch with the heavy scissors, sandpapered the spot, brushed rubber cement on it, pressed the patch down with clamps on a 2 x 4 laid between sawhorses.

I would crawl into the stacks of tires higher than myself, enjoy the rubber smell, clean, black, and smudgy. Things I liked to do when he was there, but never alone. The huge basement with the black, spidery water tank and towers of dark tires scared me when I was alone. I needed him there.

Likewise the barn. If I wanted to spend time there, it was better that he was near. There was a tombstone, a pretty little one on the top floor of the barn, which used to be the stable of the inn. Bits of straw there after all the years. Where, my father said, he sat on rafters, the beams, and caught starlings, twisted their heads off and put the heads in his pockets. There were hundreds of birds eating the grain. It was a useful game, he said.

There was the jeep, the dog, and Dad. In summer we would get up early, load the jeep with newspapers, milk, bread, cigarettes, maybe some sweet buns or tarts, and go down the cottage roads through the cedars, the branches scraping the sides of the jeep. The gravel roads to the lakefront were narrow and tunnel-like as we descended to those fairy-tale houses, the cottages.

Our house had four bedrooms upstairs and two down. My parents slept downstairs and I was allowed to sleep in whatever room I wished. Some rooms were more comforting than others and I think now it was the wallpaper. The rose room was too grown up. The blue plaid room scared me, my brother's kilt the only item hanging in the closet, the sporran waving, swaying as I walked by.

At night, around 10:30, the store would close down and I would be glad to see my parents come in for the nightly ritual of the papers, toast and tea. Maybe a game of crib.

It seemed like a very good life to me. Who could ever want to change it? And yet, I did sense that temporary feel of things. That the peace of this life, the routine of it, was too smooth somehow, too pleasurable. Underneath, never stated, was the fact that my father worked too hard. You go in and lie down, Bill, my mother would say when his breath was short, quickened.

Sometimes, when I could not find him, having gone first to the store, then to the basement, the barn, the woodshed, all the places where he worked, was most likely to be because he always worked at something, after I'd searched all these places and not found him, I would go into the unlit house. He would be lying asleep, snoozing, snoring with the paper a tent over his head or fallen to the floor, his arm limp, the fingers barely touching the floor. I would stand on the heat register opposite the couch where he slept and look at him. His hair was very thick and white and tears would come into my eyes for no reason at all. I would suddenly feel very strange, as if I were growing to understand something I could not quite understand. And I would watch him until he woke.

Part 6

·

TIME TOGETHER, TIME APART

LUCKY

Cathy Song

The baby brought us luck
from the day we brought him home.
White curtains lifted
to let in the pale lemon light.

We hung his hat on the doorknob
and raised a flag
in the shape of a fish.

The man selling corn,
the woman folding sheets,
smiled and waved their approval.
The nurse left a poem in the mailbox.

Those who visited tiptoed around
the light that had landed in our living room.
The drunk declined his usual drink.
The lady with the many bracelets

stopped her jangling in mid-gesture.
It was as if they were entering a church.

We succumbed to sleep,
the three of us and slept
through the long mornings cool
with magnolias opening beneath our window.
   His small hand curled around my thumb.
When I opened his rosebud fist, I found,
already etched, a complex map of his future.
   My breasts were sweet for days.
The smell of milk
enticed a trail of black ants
to migrate out of the Boston fern.
Like a moving signature
weaving across the carpet,
it was his first alphabet.

QUALITY TIME

Barbara Kingsolver

Miriam's one and only daughter, Rennie, wants to go to Ice Cream Heaven. This is not some vision of the afterlife but a retail establishment here on earth, right in Barrimore Plaza, where they have to drive past it every day on the way to Rennie's day-care center. In Miriam's opinion, this opportunistic placement is an example of the free-enterprise system at its worst.

"Rennie, honey, we can't today. There just isn't time," Miriam says. She is long past trying to come up with fresh angles on this argument. This is the bland, simple truth, the issue is time, not cavities or nutrition. Rennie doesn't want ice cream. She wants an angel sticker for the Pearly Gates Game, for which one only has to walk through the door, no purchase necessary. When you've collected enough stickers, you get a free banana split.

Miriam has told Rennie over and over again that she will buy her a banana split some Saturday when they have time to make an outing of it, but Rennie acts as if this has nothing to do with the matter at hand, as though she has asked for a Cabbage Patch doll and Miriam is offering to buy her shoes.

"I could just run in and run out," Rennie says after a while. "You could wait for me in the car." But she knows she has lost; the proposition is half-hearted.

"We don't even have time for that, Rennie. We're on a schedule today."

Rennie is quiet. The windshield wipers beat a deliberate, ingratiating rhythm, sounding as if they feel put-upon to be doing this job. All of southern California seems dysfunctional in the rain: cars stall, drivers go vaguely brain-dead. Miriam watches Rennie look out at the drab scenery, and wonders if for her sake they ought to live someplace with ordinary seasons—piles of raked leaves in autumn, winters with frozen streams and carrot-nosed snowmen. Someday Rennie will read about those things in books, and think they're exotic.

They pass by a brand-new auto mall, still under construction, though some of the lots are already open and ready to get down to brass tacks with anyone who'll brave all that yellow machinery and mud. The front of the mall sports a long row of tall palm trees, newly transplanted, looking frankly mortified by their surroundings. The trees depress Miriam. They were probably yanked out of some beautiful South Sea island and set down here in front of all these Plymouths and Subarus. Life is full of bum deals.

Miriam can see that Rennie is not pouting, just thoughtful. She is an extremely obliging child, considering that she's just barely five. She understands what it means when Miriam says they are "on a schedule." Today they really don't have two minutes to spare. Their dance card, so to speak, is filled. When people remark to Miriam about how well-organized she is, she laughs and declares that organization is the religion of the single parent.

It sounds like a joke, but it isn't. Miriam is faithful about the business of getting each thing done in its turn, and could no more abandon her orderly plan than a priest could swig down the transubstantiated wine and toss out wafers like Frisbees over the heads of those waiting to be blessed. Miriam's motto is that life is way too complicated to leave to chance.

But in her heart she knows what a thin veil of comfort it is that she's wrapped around herself and her child to cloak them from chaos. It all hangs on the presumption that everything has been accounted for. Most days, Miriam is a believer. The road ahead will present no serious potholes, no detour signs looming sudden and orange in the headlights, no burning barricades thrown together as reminders that the world's anguish doesn't remain mute—like the tree falling in the forest—just because no one is standing around waiting to hear it.

Miriam is preoccupied along this line of thought as she kisses Rennie goodbye and turns the steering wheel, arm over elbow, guiding her middle-aged Chevy out of the TenderCare parking lot and back onto the slick street. Her faith has been shaken by coincidence.

On Saturday, her sister Janice called to ask if she would be the guardian of Janice and Paul's three children, if the two of them should die. "We're redoing the wills," Janice reported cheerfully over the din, while in the background Miriam could hear plainly the words, "Give me that Rainbow Brite right now, dumb face."

"Just give it some thought," Janice had said calmly, but Miriam hadn't needed to think. "Will you help out with my memoirs if I'm someday the President?" her sister might as well have asked, or "What are your plans in the event of a nuclear war?" The question seemed more mythical than practical. Janice was a careful person, not given to adventure, and in any case tended to stick to those kids like some kind of maternal adhesive. Any act of God that could pick off Janice without taking the lot would be a work of outstanding marksmanship.

Late on Sunday night, while Miriam was hemming a dress of Rennie's that had fallen into favor, she'd had a phone call from her ex-husband Lute. His first cousin and her boyfriend had just been killed on a San Diego freeway by a Purolator van. Over the phone, Lute seemed obsessed with getting the logistics of the accident right, as though the way cars all obeyed the laws of physics could make this thing reasonable. The car that had the blowout was a Chrysler; the cousin and boyfriend were in her Saab; the van slammed into them from behind. "They never had a chance," Lute said, and the words chilled Miriam. Long after she went to bed she kept hearing him say "never had a chance," and imagining the pair as children. As if even in infancy their lives were already earmarked: these two will perish together in their thirties, in a Saab, wearing evening clothes, on their way to hear a friend play in the symphony orchestra. All that careful mothering and liberal-arts education gone to waste.

Lute's cousin had been a freelance cellist, often going on the road with the likes of Barry Manilow and Tony Bennett, and once, Madonna. It was probably all much tamer than it sounded. Miriam is surprised to find she has opinions about this woman, and a clear memory of her face. She only met her once, at her own wedding, when all of Lute's family had come crowding around like fog. But now this particular cousin had gained special prominence, her vague features crystallized in death, like a face on a postage stamp. Important. Someone you just can't picture doing the humdrum, silly things that life is made of—clipping her toenails or lying on the bed with her boyfriend watching *Dallas*—if you hold it clearly in your mind that she is gone.

Lute is probably crushed. He idolized her. His goal in life is to be his own boss. Freelance husbanding is just one of the things that hasn't worked out for Lute. Freelance fathering he can manage.

Miriam is thinking of Rennie while she waits through a yellow light she normally might have run. Rennie last week insisting on wearing only dresses to nursery school, and her pale, straight hair just so, with a ribbon; they'd seen *Snow White*. Rennie as a toddler standing in her crib, holding the rails, her mouth open wide with the simplest expectation you could imagine: a cookie, a game, or nothing at all, just that they would both go on being there together. Lute was already out of the picture by that time; he wouldn't have been part of Rennie's hopes. It is only lately, since she's learned to count, that Lute's absence matters to Rennie. On the Disney Channel parents come in even numbers.

The light changes and there is a honking of horns; someone has done something wrong, or too slowly, or in the wrong lane. Miriam missed it altogether, whatever it was. She remembers suddenly a conversation she had with her sister years ago when she was unexpectedly pregnant with Rennie and Janice was already a wise old mother of two. Miriam was frantic—she'd wanted a baby but didn't feel ready yet. "I haven't really worked out what it is I want to pass on to a child," she'd said to Janice, who laughed. According to Janice, parenting was three percent conscious effort and ninety-seven percent automatic pilot. "It doesn't matter what you think you're going to tell them. What matters is they're right there watching you every minute, while you let the lady with just two items go ahead of you in line, or when you lay on the horn and swear at the guy that cuts you off in traffic. There's no sense kidding yourself, what you see is what you get."

Miriam had argued that people could consciously change themselves if they tried, though in truth she'd been thinking more of Lute than herself. She remembers saying a great many things about choices and value systems and so forth, a lot of first-pregnancy high-mindedness it seems to her now. Now she understands. Parenting is something that happens mostly while you're thinking of something else.

Miriam's job claims her time for very irregular hours at the downtown branch of the public library. She is grateful that the people at Rennie's day care don't seem to have opinions about what kind of mother would work mornings one day, evenings the next. When she was first promoted to this position Miriam had a spate of irrational fears: she imagined Miss Joyce at TenderCare giving her a lecture on homemade soup and the importance of routine in the formative years. But Miss Joyce, it seems, understands modern arrangements. "The important thing is quality time," she said once to Miriam, in a way that suggested bedtime stories read with a yogic purity of concentration, a mind temporarily wiped clean of things like brake shoes and Master-Charge bills.

Miriam does try especially hard to schedule time for the two of them around Rennie's bedtime, but it often seems pointless. Rennie is likely to be absorbed in her own games, organizing animated campaigns on her bed with her stuffed animals, and finally dropping off in the middle of them, limbs askew, as though felled by a sniper.

Today is one of Miriam's afternoon-shift days. After leaving Rennie she has forty minutes in which she must do several errands before going to work. One of them is eat lunch. This is an item Miriam would actually put on a list: water African violets; do cleaners; eat lunch. She turns in at the Burger Boy and looks at her watch, surprised to see that she has just enough time to go in and sit down. Sometimes she takes the drive-through option and wolfs down a fish sandwich in the parking lot, taking large bites, rattling the ice in her Coke, unmindful of appearances. It's efficient, although it puts Miriam in mind of eating disorders.

Once she is settled inside with her lunch, her ears stray for company to the other tables, picking up scraps of other people's private talk. "More than four hundred years old," she hears, and "It was a little bit tight over the instep," and "They had to call the police to get him out of there." She thinks of her friend Bob, who is a relentless eavesdropper, though because he's a playwright he calls it having an ear for dialogue.

Gradually she realizes that at the table behind her a woman is explaining to her daughter that she and Daddy are getting a divorce. It comes to Miriam like a slow shock, building up in her nerve endings until her skin hurts. This conversation will only happen once in that little girl's life, and I have to overhear it, Miriam is thinking. It has to be *here*. The surroundings seem banal, so cheery and hygienic, so many wiped-clean plastic surfaces. But then Miriam doesn't know what setting would be better. Certainly not some unclean place, and not an expensive restaurant either—that would be worse. To be expecting a treat, only to be socked with this news.

Miriam wants badly to turn around and look at the little girl. In her mind's eye she sees Rennie in her place: small and pale, sunk back into the puffy pink of her goosedown jacket like a loaf of risen dough that's been punched down.

The little girl keeps saying, "Okay," no matter what her mother tells her.

"Daddy will live in an apartment, and you can visit him. There's a swimming pool."

"Okay."

"Everything else will stay the same. We'll still keep Peppy with us. And you'll still go to your same school."

"Okay."

"Daddy does still love you, you know."

"Okay."

Miriam is thinking that ordinarily this word would work; it has finality. When you say it, it closes the subject.

It's already dark by the time Miriam picks up Rennie at TenderCare after work. The headlights blaze accusingly against the glass doors as if it were very late, midnight even. But it's only six-thirty, and Miriam tries to cheer herself by thinking that if this were summer it would still be light. It's a trick of the seasons, not entirely her fault, that Rennie has been abandoned for the daylight hours.

She always feels more surely on course when her daughter comes back to her. Rennie bounces into the car with a sheaf of papers clutched in one fist. The paper they use at TenderCare is fibrous and slightly brown, and seems wholesome to Miriam. Like turbinado sugar, rather than refined.

"Hi, sweetie. I missed you today." Miriam leans over to kiss Rennie and buckle her in before pulling out of the parking lot. All day she has been shaky about driving, and now she dreads the trip home. All that steel and momentum. It doesn't seem possible that soft human flesh could travel through it and come out intact. Throughout the day Miriam's mind has filled spontaneously with images of vulnerable things—baby mice, sunburned eyelids, sea creatures without their shells.

"What did you draw?" she asks Rennie, trying to anchor herself.

"This one is you and me and Lute," Rennie explains. Miriam is frowning into the river of moving headlights, waiting for a break in the traffic, and feels overcome by sadness. There are so many things to pay attention to at once, and all of them so important.

"You and me and Lute," Miriam repeats.

"Uh-huh. And a dog, Pickles, and Leslie Copley and his mom. We're all going out for a walk."

A sports car slows down, letting Miriam into the street. She waves her thanks. "Would you like to go for a walk with Leslie Copley and his mom sometime?"

"No. It's just a picture."

"What would you like for supper?"

"Pot pies!" Rennie shouts. Frozen dinners are her favorite thing. Miriam rather likes them too, although this isn't something she'd admit to many people. Certainly not her mother, for instance, or to Bob, who associates processed food with intellectual decline. She wonders, though, if her privacy is an illusion. Rennie may well be revealing all the details of their home life to her nursery-school class, opening new chapters daily. What I had for dinner last night. What Mom does when we run out of socks. They probably play games along these lines at TenderCare, with entirely innocent intentions. And others, too, games with a social-worker bent: What things make you happy, or sad? What things make you feel scared?

Miriam smiles. Rennie is fearless. She does not know how it feels to be hurt, physically or otherwise, by someone she loves. The people at TenderCare probably hear a lot worse than pot pies.

"Mom," Rennie asks, "does God put things on the TV?"

"What do you mean?"

Rennie considers. "The cartoons, and the movies and things. Does God put them there?"

"No. People do that. You know how Grandpa takes movies of you with his movie camera, and then we show them on the screen? Well, it's like that. People at the TV station make the programs, and then they send them out onto your TV screen."

"I thought so," Rennie says. "Do you make them sometimes, at the library?"

Miriam hears a siren but can't tell where it's coming from. "Well, I organize programs for the library, you're right, but not TV programs. Things like storybook programs. You remember, you've come to some of those." Miriam hopes she doesn't sound irritated. She is trying to slow down and move into the right lane, because of the ambulance, but people keep passing her on both sides,

paying no attention. It makes Miriam angry. Sure enough, the ambulance is coming their way. It has to jerk to a full stop in the intersection ahead of them because of all the people who refuse to yield to the greater urgency.

"Mom, what happens when you die?"

Miriam is startled because she was thinking of Lute's poor cousin. Thinking of the condition of the body, to be exact. But Rennie doesn't even know about this relative, won't hear her sad story for years to come.

"I'm not sure, Rennie. I think maybe what happens is that you think back over your life, about all the nice things you've done and the people who've been your friends, and then you close your eyes and . . . it's quiet." She was going to say, ". . . and go to sleep," but she's read that sleep and death shouldn't be equated, that it can cause children to fear bedtime. "What do you think?"

"I think you put on your nicest dress, and then you get in this glass box and everybody cries and then the prince comes and kisses you. On the lips."

"That's what happened to Snow White, isn't it?"

"Uh-huh. I didn't like when he kissed her on the lips. Why didn't he kiss her on the cheek?"

"Well, grownups kiss on the lips. When they like each other."

"But Snow White wasn't a grownup. She was a little girl."

This is a new one on Miriam. This whole conversation is like a toboggan ride, threatening at every moment to fly out of control in any direction. She's enjoying it, though, and regrets that they will have to stop soon for some errands. They are low on produce, canned foods, aluminum foil, and paper towels, completely out of vacuum-cleaner bags and milk.

"What I think," says Miriam, after giving it some consideration, "is that Snow White was a little girl at first, but then she grew up. Taking care of the seven dwarfs helped her learn responsibility." Responsibility is something she and Rennie have talks about from time to time. She hears another siren, but this one is definitely behind them, probably going to the same scene as the first. She imagines her sister Janice's three children bundling into her life in a whirlwind of wants and possessions. Miriam doesn't even have time for another house plant. But she realizes that having time is somehow beside the point.

"So when the prince kissed her, did she grow up?" Rennie asks.

"No, before that. She was already grown up when the prince came. And they liked each other, and they kissed, and afterward they went out for a date."

"Like you and Mr. Bob?"

"Like Bob and I do sometimes, right. You don't have to call him Mr. Bob, honey. He's your friend, you can call him just Bob, if you want to."

Instead of making the tricky left turn into the shopping center, Miriam's car has gone right, flowing with the tide of traffic. It happened almost before she knew it, but it wasn't an accident. She just isn't ready to get to the grocery store, where this conversation will be lost among the bright distractions of bubble gum and soda. Looping back around the block will give them another four or five minutes. They could sit and talk in the parking lot, out of the traffic, but Miriam is starting to get her driving nerves back. And besides, Rennie would think that peculiar. Her questions would run onto another track.

"And then what happened to the seven dwarfs?" Rennie wants to know.

"I think Snow White still took care of them, until they were all grown up and could do everything by themselves."

"And did the prince help too?"

"I think he did."

"But what if Snow White died. If she stayed dead, I mean, after the prince kissed her."

Miriam now understands that this is the angle on death that has concerned Rennie all along. She is relieved. For Miriam, practical questions are always the more easily answered.

"I'm sure the dwarfs would still be taken care of," she says. "The point is that Snow White really loved them, so she'd make sure somebody was going to look after them, no matter what, don't you think?"

"Uh-huh. Maybe the prince."

"Maybe." A motorcycle dodges in front of them, too close, weaving from lane to lane just to get a few yards ahead. At the next red light they will all be stopped together, the fast drivers and the slow, shooting looks at one another as if someone had planned it all this way.

"Rennie, if something happened to me, you'd still have somebody to take care of you. You know that, don't you?"

"Uh-huh. Lute."

"Is that what you'd like? To go and live with Lute?"

"Would I have to?"

"No, you wouldn't have to. You could live with Aunt Janice if you wanted to."

Rennie brightens. "Aunt Janice and Uncle Paul and Michael-and-Donna-and-Perry?" The way she says it makes Miriam think of their Christmas card.

"Right. Is that what you'd want?"

Rennie stares at the windshield wipers. The light through the windshield is spotty, falling with an underwater strangeness on Rennie's serious face. "I'm not sure," she says. "I'll have to think it over."

Miriam feels betrayed. It depresses her that Rennie is even willing to take the question seriously. She wants her to deny the possibility, to give her a tearful hug and say she couldn't live with anyone but Mommy.

"It's not like I'm sending you away, Rennie. I'm not going to die while you're a little girl. We're just talking about what-if. You understand that, right?"

"Right," Rennie says. "It's a game. We play what-if at school." After another minute she says, "I think Aunt Janice."

They are repeating their route now, passing again by the Burger Boy where Miriam had lunch. The tables and chairs inside look neater than it's possible to keep things in real life, and miniature somehow, like doll furniture. It looks bright and safe, not the sort of place that could hold ghosts.

On an impulse Miriam decides to put off the errands until tomorrow. She feels reckless, knowing that tomorrow will already be busy enough without a backlog. But they can easily live another day without vacuum cleaner bags and she'll work out something about the milk.

We could stop here and have a hamburger for dinner," Miriam says. "Or a fish sandwich. And afterward we could stop for a minute at Ice Cream Heaven. Would you like that?"

"No. Pot pies!"

"And no Ice Cream Heaven?"

"I don't need any more angel stickers. Leslie Copley gave me twelve."

"Well, that was nice of him."

"Yep. He hates bananas."

"Okay, we'll go straight home. But do you remember that pot pies take half an hour to cook in the oven? Will you be too hungry to wait, once we get home?"

"No, I'll be able to wait," Rennie says, sounding as if she really will. In the overtones of her voice and the way she pushes her blonde hair over her shoulder there is a startling maturity, and Miriam is frozen for a moment with a vision of a much older Rennie. All the different Rennies—the teenager, the adult—are already contained in her hands and her voice, her confidence. From moments like these, parents can find the courage to believe in the resilience of their children's lives. They will barrel forward like engines, armored by their own momentum, more indestructible than love.

"Okay, then, pot pies it is," Miriam says. "Okay."

UNMASKED

Calvin Trillin

We didn't do Halloween this year. Oh, sure, I got out my axe-murderer's mask, in case I wanted to march in the parade that's traditional in our neighborhood. But we didn't have our usual post-parade party. We didn't hang a witch piñata out of the window. When a friend of mine who lives in another city asked why, I offered a simple answer: "We plumb ran out of kids."

The friend—I'll call him Horace—knew what I was talking about. He has run out of kids himself, and his neighborhood doesn't even have a Halloween parade that can accommodate unaccompanied grownups. A couple of years ago, he suggested to his youngest daughter that it might be nice to celebrate Halloween the way they had done in the past, and she informed him that it was not customary for third-year law students to go trick-or-treating.

"That's what it's like here, too," I said to Horace. I told him about how we had to give up our Easter-egg hunt several years back.

"But you must have held that Easter-egg hunt for fifteen years!" Horace said.

It's true that when our kids got too old to search for Easter eggs themselves we managed to extend the hunt a few years by having them serve as guides and bearers for some of the younger kids on the block. Finally, though, we had to call a halt.

"Why?" Horace asked. "What happened?"

"Same as Halloween," I said. "We plumb ran out of kids."

When Horace's kids were small, he's told me, he loved taking them around the neighborhood to trick-or-treat. He enjoyed the opportunity to have a little chat with neighbors he sometimes didn't get to talk to from one year to the next. It was always fun to see what each child had chosen as a costume—a witch, a Mars bar, Big Bird—and, Horace admitted to me, he rather liked getting into his own costume. He was a pirate captain. He approached each house shouting "Avast, ye hearties!" If his gang ran across people who offered apples or granola or whole-grain sugarless biscuits, or anything other than the disgusting teeth-rotters that Horace thought proper for Hallow-een, he threatened to run them through.

All that is over now. On October 31st, Horace and his wife sit home, recalling ghosts of Halloweens past. Even the occasional visit of trick-or-treaters doesn't do much to cheer them up. Horace still likes to see the neighborhood kids in their costumes, but he finds himself so envious of the accompanying adults that it's difficult to muster much cheerfulness.

A year ago, his wife suggested that he might feel better if he wore his old pirate-captain costume when he opened the door to trick-or-treaters, but a little boy in the first group of callers—a four-year-old who was fero-ciously costumed as a snaggletoothed monster—burst into tears at the sight of him. Now Horace wears his cardigan, which he was hoping would make him feel like Mr. Rogers but somehow makes him feel more like Mr. Wilson, the grump who lives next door to Dennis the Menace.

Horace and I agree about what's causing the problem for us and a lot of our contemporaries. Not long after you run out of your own kids to take trick-or-treating—or to take to the zoo or to the ballgame or fishing—you're supposed to have grandchildren to replace them. But there are no grandchildren in sight. When you read about the effects of changing marriage and child-bearing patterns in this country—women waiting until after their careers have taken hold before they get married, for instance, or couples living together for years before making it official and having kids—what you don't read about is that this is causing what can only be called a grandchildren gap.

This is why Horace spent this past Halloween at home in his cardigan, feeling like Mr. Wilson. He understands that. He understands that twenty years ago someone the age of his youngest daughter would probably have been the mother of two instead of being an assistant district attorney. Horace wants his daughter to do whatever makes her happy. He's proud of her. He has every reason to believe that she is a terrific assistant district attorney. On the other hand, he misses his pirate-captain costume.

TRAVELING ISN'T CHILD'S PLAY

Roger Yepsen

I taped a big road map of Italy to our kitchen wall. Each day I asked our children to point out the spots where we would be staying. Roma, Gubbio, Sicilia. Friends warned us that the kids were a little young for a backpacking adventure—Rhodes, just 3, and Metthea, 5. But Ali and I were eager to get back into the country that had intoxicated us on an earlier, childless trip.

My first premonition of trouble came before we took off. Rhodes somehow managed to take four significant falls on the seamless, one-level floors of the airport. I couldn't keep from forecasting the number of accidents we might expect over the next two months of medieval steps and volcanic slopes.

An hour off the plane, leaving Rome's central rail terminal, we were accosted by beggars. They were about the size of our kids, but up close I could see that they were tiny, wizened teen-agers. I tried to keep Rhodes and Metthea away from their outstretched arms—covered, for a reason I couldn't fathom at the moment, by newspapers.

Then they abruptly scampered away, and I knew even before swatting my rump for confirmation, that I had just lost my wallet.

With kids in tow, standing on an island in the middle of rush-hour traffic, I couldn't give chase. I felt like a parent on a class trip that would never end.

The feeling persisted. Our budget dictated that we share a single room each night. We dined together, even napped and went to bed at the same times. After a couple of weeks of this, I developed a scratchy feeling. It's a reaction I get to groups, even when they happen to share my last name. (As a teenager during the Cuban missile crisis, I didn't fear annihilation half as much as the prospect of spending months with my family in the cinderblock cube my dad was building in the basement.)

As with other parents who work away from home, I suspect, my love for my kids was keenest in the abstract—when checking on them at night, or listening to their tiny, disembodied voices over the phone. Now, in Italy, I was smothered by round-the-clock in-the-face fatherhood. I had lost my identity to what I came to think of as the family beast. This ungainly animal had eight legs of various lengths, four stomachs and four bladders. It was not of a single mind about anything, which explained why the simplest decisions might flare up into contests of will.

Rhodes discovered that, as owner of two of the family beast's legs, he could lobby for a gelato or whatever else he wanted simply by becoming immobile. We would be walking through a town and I'd suddenly notice that he was half a block back, frozen to the sidewalk, expressionless, oblivious to the fond looks and pats of passers-by. Fortunately, a 3-year-old is relatively portable—relative to, say, a 12-year-old. I couldn't droop him over my shoulder because of the pack, so I held him before me, facing front, as if bearing an icon in a religious parade. (The sight must have been heart-wrenching. In our five experiences with hitchhiking, only one car failed to stop.)

Hassles like these were bearable. They're the stuff of good stories, after all, and one good story is worth a carousel of slides. More worrisome was that I somehow had misplaced any sense of being in a foreign country. I hadn't even taken my sketchbook or camera out of the pack. At first I blamed this emotional flatness on my age. Then I blamed my kids.

Young children don't know what "foreign" means, I realized in a bit of an epiphany. They don't discriminate between over here and over there. To Rhodes and Metthea, Italy was a lot like home, only without lawns. We would be walking around a strange city, and they'd swear they saw the back of a neighbor's house.

On the other hand, I *demanded* foreignness. On my first trip, I wasn't happy when I found myself around other Americans, or saw young Italians dining on hamburgers and Coca-Cola instead of pizza and vino locale. And here I was dragging my own domesticity around by the hand. The kids neutralized any flavor of intrigue before I could capture it in a postcard or photograph. Wherever we four went was home, and home was a place I had been intent on escaping.

Matters bottomed out one morning in Sicily, as we hiked the wildflower-strewn path to the lonely Greek temple of Seggesta. Its stone columns rose high above us like the bleached bones of a dead culture.

I felt satisfactorily moved by the place. But what were the kids looking at? What kids always look at on walks: weirdly shaped pebbles, candy wrappers, bits of broken glass.

I grasped Rhodes's chin and forced him to acknowledge the columns. "Very, extremely old!" I said. But he didn't sense anything mystical about Seggesta. And standing beside him, I realized with a heavy feeling in my gut that I no longer did either.

I was rescued by an extinct volcano on one of the Aeolian islands, just off the Sicilian coast. It was a cloud-capped party hat of a mountain, looming over our pensione. It dared me to come on up, in a way that no mountain ever had.

I picked up a topographic map at the local bar, along with plenty of free advice on the fastest way to the top. While the rest of the family settled down for the daily nap, I packed a little bottle of the island's red wine and a breadboard-sized block of Perugina chocolate.

As I climbed above the olive groves that cloak the island's lower slopes, a sharp wind began shoving my body this way and that. I recalled reading that these islands were named for Aeolus, the wind god. Holding on to my glasses to keep them from blowing off my head, I looked up to see his breath shredding the clouds at the summit. Then I took a closer look at the map, at the dashes that the bar regulars said marked the beeline trail to the peak. The key revealed that the line wasn't a trail at all, but the political boundary between two townships.

Ahead of me rose hundreds of giant steps—10-foot-high stone walls that centuries ago had been carved out of the mountain's perfect geometry in order to grow grapes, capers and olives. The skinny fields were abandoned to briars, which had managed to raise an inch-high nap on my new Banana Republic sweater.

By the time I reached the top, what was a pleasant, T-shirt sort of day at sea level had become something of a winter gale. The term "hypothermia" popped into my head. I had to scuttle like a crab to avoid being peeled off the mountain altogether. I found shelter on the leeward side of a boulder, and with cold-stiffened fingers managed to unwrap the chocolate and uncork the wine. Nibbling and sipping, I looked out at my prize—a view of the sea, its translucent aqua scratched here and there by the wake of a hydrofoil ferry. I could make out the purple triangles of other Aeolian islands.

I located the little white chip within which my family now would be getting up from their naps. A long, invisible tether ran from me to that building, but I felt that the climb had given it a good stretching.

THE WAY BACK HOME:
REVISITING MY GRANDFATHER

Eric Latzky

New York City, July 1990: I came home. Death? Rebirth? The end of an exile? Maybe it was just having lived outside my natural habitat for too long. After living in Los Angeles for nearly five years, I knew more about why I left the place where I was born than why I decided to return.

I took the red-eye. The flight landed at six in the morning, I dropped off my bags at my mother's apartment, nearly at the bottom of Manhattan, and went directly up to the Bronx, where I'm from. There, at Montefiore Hospital, Louis, my grandfather, was about to undergo emergency open-heart surgery. I arrived just in time to see a nurse inject a needleful of morphine into his arm. My family—my grandmother, my uncle, my mother, my brother—turned away, horrified. I watched. I think it was the first time in years Louis had felt something other than pain.

Four. I have just caught my first fish. We are at the lake near the pink bungalow in Denville, New Jersey, but down at the far end away from where the people swim, near where the trees start. It's dark inside where the trees are, it's scary, but also I wonder what's in there. It's early Sunday morning. There is no one else around, just me and Louis. I look like this: my hair is cut in bangs and I am wearing my striped overalls, rolled up past my knees so I can go in the water. It's not sunny out; it's kind of smoky. The water is calm. I have my black fishing pole that Louis got me. It is more than two times taller than me, and it has a reel that I can cast with, and a red-and-white bob. I think Louis put a worm on the hook, which is how I got the fish, a gray lake fish that I am holding up above my head, still on the hook, with my left hand. I'm holding the pole with my right. I look a little mad. Louis says I should throw it back because it's too small, but I won't do it. I stand there until he takes the picture.

Louis survived the operation. The surgeon thought it was incredible how well he did, how strong he was, considering his age.

For fifty years, Louis worked as a purveyor, buying meat out of Little West Twelfth Street wholesale meat market, an area of a few square blocks near the river, and making deliveries to his clients, restaurants in and around the city. He would go to work at four in the morning, make all his purchases—sides of beef, legs of lamb, endless provisions—by six or so, and get everything delivered by eight, before the rest of the city even got started. I used to go to work with him from the time I was very young.

I didn't know then what the strange triangle-shaped building in the middle of the market was. Not too many years later I would come to know it as the Anvil, the notoriously historic gay bar. Nor did I know, as a boy, that this area surrounding what I simply called the meat market—rows of nineteenth-century town houses, cobblestone streets, and, closer to the river, industrial warehouses and seemingly abandoned piers—had such an eloquent double meaning. I didn't know that it was actually a neighborhood with a name, the West Village, and that it was the center of New York's gay world, a place where I would later spend a fair amount of time.

●   ●   ●

Eight. The sun is just coming up around the West Side Highway, the part of it that's still standing. I'm cold; it's not winter anymore, but it's not really spring yet either. It smells like meat. We are in the old green truck. It's bumpy because of the cobblestone streets. Joe is driving. Michael, my brother, is sitting on the crate. I'm on the seat, high up so I can see out. Louis, like always, is riding half outside the open door, wearing his cowboy hat. It's a Stetson. I know because he let me try it on once, even though it was bigger than my whole head. Louis tells Joe to pull over for a minute. He wants to run into a place to see if he can get a special cut of something a client needs. He tells us to wait. The sky is orange, streaked with clouds. Across the street, a man comes out of the triangle-shaped building and walks in the direction of the truck. When he gets close, I can see he has what looks like a diamond in his ear. It's sparkling. I look at it, then I look at the man, right into his eyes. He looks at me. When I realize that our eyes are looking directly at each other, it makes me turn away.

With no plan in mind, completely disoriented and kind of shocked, I went to live with two friends in SoHo. I spent the summer on the subway, back and forth between their apartment and the Bronx—first the IRT to Jerome Avenue until Louis was discharged from the hospital there, then the Broadway local to 231st Street in Riverdale, near my grandparents' apartment. Those long, air-conditioned rides were what really, finally brought me back to New York—every site, every image of my childhood came into and then went out of focus through the windows of the elevated subway cars. They were like giant TV screens moving constantly, playing reruns of the same old show over and over.

Louis began to recover, slowly. He didn't seem to want to talk much; he seemed distant, inside himself, the opposite of the way he had always been. We sat on the terrace of my grandparents' apartment surrounded by thickly greened treetops limiting the view to a small, comfortable, familiar distance. It was quiet, breezy. We watched the summer rainstorms. Louis read the paper, did the crosswords as he had all his life. We didn't say too much to each other. Perhaps it was enough for him just to have me around.

•   •   •

Nine. Papa Harry, my other grandfather, died last night. My father said that means I won't ever be able to see him again, except one more time. It's early in the morning. We're at this place called Hirsch & Sons, down near the end of the Grand Concourse. All of my family, I mean everyone, is coming here. They're all being really nice to me, and to my brother, and to Marc and Scott, my cousins. I'm all dressed up, and I think people are crying, the big people, and it smells like some kind of chemical or something in here. I don't know what it is. My father comes over and says we can go see Papa Harry now and he takes us into this room. When we get up

close to the box Papa Harry is lying in, I can see his face is white and his eyes are closed, but not like he's sleeping. He's wearing a suit. I don't want to keep looking, but my father says I have to, at least for a few minutes. As soon as he lets me, I go outside; Michael and Marc and Scott go too. Then—I don't know why—I start crying, really loud, and I can't breathe almost, but I can't stop. Louis comes over and he takes my hand. I tell him that I don't want to go back in there. He says I don't have to and, when everyone else goes back in, he takes me for a long walk in the neighborhood. We walk by a pet store and in the window there's a fish tank. There are no fish in it, but there's a tiny stingray. It's amazing, the way it glides through the water, the way the tail follows. It looks like when I fly my kite, but under water. Louis asks me if I want him to buy it for me. He's still holding my hand. I tell him no, I just want to look at it.

The summer passed. By August, Louis seemed ready to leave the familiar comfort of the terrace, to begin to get back out somewhat. There were moments when it would occur to him that he could do things now that he hadn't been able to do without pain for years. We drove the car a little, we shopped for groceries, once or twice we went out for a meal.

He was cautious, unsure. The first time we drove he had me sit next to him. After just a few blocks he said that maybe I should drive. I asked how he was feeling. I thought perhaps it was too much of a strain, that turning the wheel was even too difficult. The doctors had said he would be sore for a while. I thought, maybe, he wasn't ready to be doing this. But still, he wasn't talking much, as if he wanted you to know what he was thinking. He would motion with his fingers and half expect you to understand. I said, "Louis, I don't know what it is you're trying to say." He said he was feeling all right. I said in that case I wouldn't drive.

Twelve. We are going to Florida today—Miami Beach. It's Christmas vacation. I have never flown in an airplane before. Neither has Michael. I can't believe you can be in one place now, where it's really cold and snowing, and a few hours later be in a place where it's warm enough to go to the beach, even go swimming. I want to see what a real palm tree looks like. The flight's not until four in the afternoon, but it's beginning to look like a blizzard outside and Louis is getting nervous. It's only about ten-thirty in the morning, but he says we should go to the airport now. I guess he thinks we won't be able to get there at all if we wait. Everything's packed, so we just get in the car and go. We get there quickly, maybe it takes an hour or so. The flight is leaving from this special charter terminal, and there's not a whole lot to do. Michael and I get candy, we run around, we watch these little pay TVs that are pretty cool because we can each watch what we want and for once we don't have to fight about it. Around two they make an announcement that the flight is being delayed, because of the snow I guess. They say it won't leave until seven at night. Michael and I

start to kind of fight. We start out playing, but like always Michael gets mad, and then he gets really mean. He always ends up winning, which he can do because he's bigger than me—by less than two years, but still, he's bigger. I guess we're making a lot of noise or something because the next thing I know Louis is right there and we both get hit. Then we're quiet for a while. The flight takes off at about eight. When the plane starts to move fast down the runway, I can't believe it; it's not like anything I've ever felt. It's like there's a hole of air in my stomach. I smile and look at Louis. My grandfather is sitting next to me.

In SoHo, we kept the air conditioner going most of the time, but every once in a while we would rough it. On those nights, I would lie in bed, sleepless, late into the night, sweating, naked, wondering what would happen. To my grandfather. To me, my new life back in New York. I wondered what I would do. Not constantly, but sometimes, I would think, maybe this is it. Maybe I've lost the ability to live. Maybe, now that I've made it back home, this is the end after all.

One Sunday, like many others, I took the subway up to the Bronx for a visit. But there was no answer when I rang the buzzer. I rang it again. Nothing. It's strange, I thought, that they would go somewhere without me, without at least telling me. Especially because they knew I was coming. I went to a diner around the corner, drank coffee, ate breakfast, tried to figure it out. I called down to SoHo to see if there was a message, I called the hospital, I sat there. I wondered. After about an hour, I tried the hospital again—the emergency room this time. That was it. When I got there, half my family had reconvened. It wasn't catastrophic; the doctor wasn't sure what it was, and by four Louis had been discharged and we all went home.

My family dispersed, my grandmother relaxed a bit, Louis and I sat on the terrace. Louis seemed to be talking more about death than anything else. It didn't seem strange though, perhaps because it seemed natural to me that one would want to contemplate the subject. Somehow we began to talk about my cousin Harold who had died of AIDS about a year and a half earlier.

I think Louis was trying to say something to me that afternoon, something, perhaps, he thought I could understand better than the others. Louis and I never had the language to discuss big things directly. As his friends began to die throughout the eighties, he would tell me of the deaths but never what it was like, what it meant to lose someone you knew, cared about.

He became quiet for a while. We sat there on the terrace, surrounded by the trees, into the evening. I think that Louis was cherishing the summer. He never turned to me, didn't look at me directly when he spoke. "It's a shame," he said quietly, almost like his thoughts were dreams, "all those handsome, talented men dying so young."

Twenty. It's Thanksgiving. I'm packing. Tomorrow I'm leaving for Europe. Actually I'm going to travel through Italy and Switzerland, then on to Austria. In Vienna I'll get a train into the Ukraine, and then on to Moscow. My other grandmother, Dora, still has family there; I'm going to meet them for the first time. I have plans to go to Leningrad also. Eventually, I'll head back through Berlin, maybe some other places, Amsterdam or wherever, and at some point I'll land in Paris. At this moment I have no plans to return to the States. On the outside, Louis has been saying things that make me think he doesn't want me to go, that maybe I won't make it, that's the way he puts it. Make it, he says, as if I haven't. Those words keep running through my mind. I've been out on my own since I was eighteen, and out of the closet since I was fifteen, but I guess he hasn't seen too much of that. I guess I haven't let him. After dinner we sit down on a couch together. Louis has an old photo album in his hand that he wants me to see. He doesn't say much; we just sit together and he turns the pages, telling me where each photo was taken and when. First there are a few in New York. He's wearing a long beaver coat and he has his foot up on the runner of a Stutz Bearcat Roadster—I think that was the name of it. It has no top. He says the car was his and he kind of starts to smile when he says it but just a little. Then there are a whole series of photographs taken in South America: Rio de Janeiro, Buenos

Aires, a bunch of different places. He says he sailed there on a steamship from New York. He is so handsome and cool-looking in the photos. He looks like a gangster, like that old movie star that played gangsters—George Raft. When he closes the photo album he doesn't look at me, but he tells me he was exactly my age when he took that trip.

Louis's health fluctuated. Some days he felt all right, other days not so well. He continued to move further and further inside himself. He sat on the terrace, he read the paper, we talked a little but not too much. Overall, it appeared as though he was getting better.

September came, the weather moved into that teasing period where the hint of fall is always in the air and somehow, still, it feels as hot and unpleasant as it had for the last three months. Gilda, my mother, had been talking to my great-aunt Rose, Louis's sister, about throwing a birthday party for Louis, to celebrate his health, but perhaps even more to help him see that life goes on, that he'd be okay. That was the thing he had the most trouble believing. A party would be something he could look forward to. It would suggest that he could begin to make plans again, to continue his life on more than just a moment-to-moment basis.

Gilda and Rose decided to go ahead. It was to be about fifteen of us. At first they thought it would be better to have a private room, someplace where it would be just us, but in the end they booked a huge table at a large, busy, well-known restaurant uptown, on the east side. I think they wanted people to see us celebrate, to see us be happy, as if in doing so it would confirm that we were, in fact, and that everything here was just fine.

Gilda and Michael and I decided to get Louis a gift together. We sent away to New Mexico for a kachina, a Hopi doll. Louis had talked, for some time, about wanting to own one. The doll arrived, full of complicated detail, as did the date. Michael flew in from Los Angeles yet one more time. Everyone dressed as if it were a wedding: suits, dresses, jewels, shiny shoes. Despite all the difficulties—endless feuds, ancient stalemates, serious health questions, absent members—we looked like a family. We sat together, we laughed, we toasted, we feasted, we put our differences aside and spent an evening together celebrating Louis's birthday. He was happy that night, as was my grandmother, Claire, everyone really, even if we weren't necessarily happy together.

Was it one week or two, or only a matter of days after the birthday party? I don't remember exactly, though if I looked at a calendar I could pinpoint the date, that I know. It was Yom Kippur, the most religious holiday of the year for Jews, if you're religious. The call came at two that Saturday morning. I was sleeping but woke up instantly; the moment the phone rang, I jumped right off the futon in my friends' place in SoHo. The moment the phone rang, I knew it was the end. I knew it before I even picked it up. "I'm sorry to wake you," my mother's voice was shaking, scared. "Louis died tonight."

Things happened quickly. It was only a matter of moments before I was dressed and in a taxi with Gilda and her brother Harold. Very shortly, we were in the Bronx, my grandmother was crying, people were being called, arrangements were being made. Jews don't wait; they bury the dead immediately. Which isn't easy on a holiday when, according to the religion, you're not even supposed to turn on a light.

The following morning, little more than twenty-four hours later, a limousine arrived. We climbed in wearing dark clothing, silent except for crying and breaths, and drove across the Bronx to the old neighborhood, the place where Louis and Claire had spent half their lives, where they had raised Gilda and Harold, where they had grown older, more comfortable, until they moved to Riverdale, to the apartment with the terrace that Louis loved so much.

The funeral parlor on the Grand Concourse was covered in graffiti, the parking lot surrounded by barbed wire. But if it weren't for these outward signs, it could've been a moment from any number of days in my childhood. Rooms full of people arrived, people who had known Louis forever.

The immediate family was called in to view the body. My beating heart was in my throat as I walked through the door, but I made myself be strong. I made myself stand up and do it. How many deaths had I been present at in the last decade, I asked myself. Why was this one any different? I walked up to the casket and there was Louis, my grandfather, lying still, in a burial shroud. He looked small, angelic. How could it be? He looked like a young man, like the gangster, the man in the photo with his foot up on the car. I remember the rabbi saying that for the father to die on such a day, on Yom Kippur, that it was surely a mitzvah, a blessing for the whole family.

I took a breath, put my hand first on the side of the casket and let it rest there for a minute. I closed my eyes, let out the breath, opened my eyes, and then I did it. I put my hands to Louis's cheek and kept it there, the cheek that I had kissed so many times in his life, in mine, the same cheek that boy had kissed—the boy in bangs with a fishing pole refusing to throw back a too-small fish; the boy in his grandfather's Stetson hat; the boy about to fly in an airplane for the very first time; the boy who cried after seeing his grandfather dead in a box.

MY MOTHER, THE PHOTOGRAPHER

Garnette Mullis

The shade, the light were not easily managed.
Despite snags in arranging her children,
my mother planned entire albums of events
to bind us all together in time.
Here, two are seated, two stand,
Here, the girls wear hats, the boys jackets.
Here, my brothers grin, my sister's smile blurs,
My mother's precision
placed us in these clusters.

I remember her waving her arms
until our group satisfied her ideas for a family
then moving the camera from her right hand
to her left until we all held still.

She could not see
that our separate visions met only for a moment
at the dark boundary of her body.
She could not know the way her features,
the texture of her dress
would fade out of the sunlight,
leaving a pose to steady our glances.

There are no photographers among her children,
I search again from snapshot to snapshot
for the shadow she must have cast,
It is nowhere on these pages of photographs.

ABOUT THE CONTRIBUTORS

JUDY BLUNT's first book of poetry *Not Quite Stone* won the 1992 Merriam Frontier Award. A book of essays is forthcoming from Little, Brown & Co. in 1996. She lives and works in Missoula, Montana.

DIANE FASSEL is a writer and an organizational consultant. Her three books are *The Addictive Organization*, *Working Ourselves to Death*, and *Growing Up Divorced*.

PETE FROMM has published the story collections *The Tall Uncut* and *King of the Mountain*, the novel *Monkey Tag*, and the autobiographical *Indian Creek Chronicles*, which is winner of the Pacific Northwest Booksellers 1994 Book Award. "Helmets" is from a collection-in-progress, *Dutch Elm*.

PAMELA GEMIN is a Michigan native whose poems have appeared in such journals as *Bellowing Ark*, *Calyx*, *Primavera*, and *The Spoon River Poetry Review*. She teaches English at The University of Wisconsin-Oshkosh.

NIKKI GIOVANNI was nominated for the National Book Award in 1973 for *Gemini: An Extended Autobiographical Statement*. Her most recent books include *Vacation Time*, *Those Who Ride the Night Winds* and *Spin a Soft Black Song*. She is a professor of English at Virginia Tech.

ELLEN GOODMAN worked for *Newsweek*, *Detroit Free Press*, and the *Boston Globe*. In 1980, she won the Pulitzer Prize for commentary. Since 1976, she has been a syndicated columnist with Washington Post Writers Group. Her published works are *Turning Points*, *Close to Home*, and *At Large*.

TZIVIA GOVER is an MFA candidate in Creative Nonfiction at Columbia University. Her poetry and prose have appeared in a number of journals including *Peregrine* and *The Evergreen Chronicles*, and anthologies including *The Femme Mystique*, edited by Leslea Newman.

JANE HOWARD began her career as a *Life* magazine reporter and editor and received the Friends of Literature Award in 1974 for *A Different Woman*. In 1978, she published *Families*, which the *New York Times* critic John Leonard observed is "crowded with likable people of all ages trying to cope in groups with the fact of knifelike individuality." Her most recent book is *Margaret Mead: A Life*.

JULIA KASDORF received the Thomas Wolfe Memorial Prize for Poetry at New York University. Her first book, *Sleeping Preacher*, won the 1991 Agnes Lynch Starrett Poetry Prize.

BARBARA KINGSOLVER's previous books include the novels *Pigs in Heaven*, *Animal Dreams*, *The Bean Trees*, the short story collection *Homeland and Other Stories*, and other works of fiction, nonfiction, and poetry. She lives with her daughter in Tucson, Arizona.

GALWAY KINNELL's *Selected Poems*, published in 1982, won both the National Book Award and the Pulitzer Prize. His most recent collection of poetry is *When One Has Lived A Long Time Alone*. A former MacArthur fellow, Galway Kinnell is former State Poet of Vermont and Samuel F. B. Morse Professor of Arts and Science at New York University.

NORBERT KRAPF is the author of the poetry collection *Somewhere in Southern Indiana* and the forthcoming *Blue-Eyed Grass: Poems of Germany*. He lives with his wife and children in Roslyn Heights, New York, and teaches at Long Island University.

MAXINE KUMIN, the former Poet-Laureate for New Hampshire and the Pulitzer Prize Winner for Poetry in 1973, has published ten volumes of poetry, as well as novels, short stories, and essays on country living. Her most recent collections include *Looking for Luck*, *Nurture*, and *The Long Approach*.

ERIC LATZKY's essays and articles have appeared in the anthologies *A Member of the Family* and *Friends and Lovers*, both edited by John Preston, and in publications including *The Los Angeles Times*, *Los Angeles Weekly*, *Interview*, and *Bomb*. His novel, *Three Views from Vertical Cliffs*, was published in 1991. Having lived in Paris and Los Angeles, he now makes his home in New York City where he was born.

AL MAGINNES's poetry has been published in *Poetry*, *Antioch Review*, *Georgia Review*, and many other national and regional journals. In 1991, *Nightshade Press* published a chapbook of his poems entitled *Outside a Tattoo Booth*. He lives in Raleigh, North Carolina.

PAUL MARTIN is the recipient of a poetry fellowship from the Pennsylvania Council of the Arts. He has one collection of his poetry *Green Tomatoes* (Heatherstone Press) and has been published in *Kansas Quarterly*, *Southern Poetry Review*, *Louisville Review*, and *Yankee*. He lives in Ironton, Pennsylvania.

DONNA MASINI's *That Kind of Danger* won her the 1993 Barnard New Women's Poets Prize. Her poems have appeared in *Paris Review, Georgia Review, Parnassus, Boulevard, Pequod,* and many other journals. She lives in New York City and teaches at the Writer's Voice.

KEVIN ELLIOT MILAM lives with her husband and two daughters, Clare (5 1/2 years) and Frances (3 months), in Seattle, Washington. Her poems have appeared in *Mothering, Pleiades, Portland Review, The Seattle Review,* and others.

SUE MILLER lives and writes in Cambridge, Massachusetts. She is the author of three best-selling novels: *For Love, Family Pictures,* and *The Good Mother.*

AURORA LEVINS MORALES, the author of fiction, essays, poetry, and documentary scripts and plays, has published in *Ms., The American Voice, La Nuez,* and *Callaloo.* In 1986, she co-authored with her mother *Getting Home Alive.*

GARNETTE MULLIS was a native of Pine Bluff, Arkansas, and a graduate of the MFA Writing Program at the University of Arkansas. She lived and worked in New York before returning to Pine Bluff, where she died of breast cancer in the winter of 1991.

BOBBIE SUE NADAL, a transplanted Californian, has earned an MFA in writing from Vermont College. Poet, critic, essayist, and teacher, her work recently appeared in *The Harvard Review, The Pittsburgh Quarterly,* and *The Dallas Review.* She now lives in Texas.

MARY HELEN PONCE is the author of *Taking Control,* a collection of stories, and *The Wedding,* a novel published by Arte Publico Press. Her stories have been widely published in literary reviews and magazines.

ANNA QUINDLEN is the Pulitzer Prize-winning columnist whose column appeared twice weekly in *The New York Times* and was syndicated in other papers. She is the author of collections of her columns, *Thinking Out Loud* and *Living Out Loud,* and one novel, *Object Lessons,* published in 1991.

MARIANN RITZER grew up with ten brothers and sisters, no pets, and a Catholic church that loomed high on a hill near Lake Michigan shores. She combines these childhood images with fiction in her first collection of poems *An Evening on Mildred Street.*

PATTIANN ROGERS's most recent book *Firekeeper: New and Selected Poems* contains selections from her five poetry books, *The Expectations of Light, The Tattooed Lady in the Garden, Legendary Performance, Splitting and Binding,* and *Geocentric.* The recipient of two NEA grants, a Guggenheim Fellowship, and a Lannan Poetry Fellowship, Pattiann Rogers has won many prizes for her work, including four Pushcart Prizes. She is the mother of two grown sons and lives with her husband, a geophysicist, in Colorado.

JEAN RYSSTAD lives in Prince Rupert, British Columbia. *Traveling In,* her collection of short fiction, explores family relationships within the commercial fishing industry on the north coast of Canada.

DENNIS SALEH's most recent book of poems, *This is Not Surrealism*, won the first chapbook competition from Willamette River Books.

ESMERALDA SANTIAGO is the author of the best-selling memoir *When I Was Puerto Rican*. Her writing has appeared in *The New York Times*, *The Boston Globe*, *The Christian Science Monitor*, and *Vista* magazine. She lives with her husband and two children in Boston.

NAN SAVILLE lives in Greenwich Village, where she has been a member of the faculty and administrative staff at her alma mater, New York University, for over fifteen years. Her work has appeared in several anthologies, including *Erotic Noire* and *Homespun Images*.

CATHY SONG's poetry books include *Frameless Windows*, *Squares of Light* and *Picture Bride*. She lives with her husband and son in Honolulu, Hawaii.

SANDI SONNENFELD holds degrees from Mt. Holyoke College and the University of Washington. Her work has appeared in numerous periodicals including *This Sojourner*, *Emrys Journal*, and the British anthology *Sex and the City*. Sandi was recently named a national finalist for the David Dornstein Memorial Creative Writing Contest sponsored by The Coalition for the Advancement of Jewish Education.

BARBARA STERN is a psychotherapist, parent educator, and single mother of 5-year-old Jenna.

PATTI TANA is the author of three books of poetry, most recently *Wetlands*, and is a Professor of English at Nassau Community College (SUNY) in New York.

LUCI TAPAHONSO has published three books of poetry, *One More Shiprock Night*, *Seasonal Woman*, and *A Breeze Swept Through*. Born in Shiprock, New Mexico, she is a member of the Navajo Nation and an assistant professor of English at the University of Kansas in Lawrence, Kansas, where she lives with her husband and children.

SUE ELLEN THOMPSON is a poet and freelance writer living in Mystic, Connecticut. Her first book, *This Body of Silk*, won the 1986 Samuel French Morse Prize. *The Wedding Boat*, her second book, was published by Owl Creek Press in 1995.

RICHARD TILLINGHAST is the author of five books of poetry: *Sleep Watch*, *The Knife and Other Poems*, *Sewanee in Ruins*, *Our Flag Was Still There*, and *The Stonecutter's Hand*. He teaches in the Master of Fine Arts program at the University of Michigan and lives in Ann Arbor.

CALVIN TRILLIN is a staff writer for *The New Yorker* and the author of eighteen titles, the most recent of which are *Travels With Alice*, *Enough's Enough*, *American Stories*, *Remembering Denny*, *Deadline Poet*, and *Too Soon To Tell*. He lives in New York City.

JOHN UPDIKE is the author of sixteen novels, six collections of poetry, and more than twenty other titles, including short story collections, essays and criticism, and children's books. His most recent collection of short stories *The Afterlife and Other*

Stories was published in 1995. Born and raised in Shillington, Pennsylvania, he has made his home in Massachusetts since 1957. He is the father of four children and the grandfather of three boys.

SUSAN VREELAND's first novel, *What Love Sees,* is under development as a CBS television movie, and her short fiction has appeared in *Crosscurrents, Kalliope, Sistersong,* and *Ambergris.* She is currently at work on a second novel, *When Cedars Make Strong Talk.*

ROGER WEINGARTEN is the author of eight books of poetry, including *Ghost Wrestling* and *Infant Bonds of Joy,* published by David R. Godine. He teaches in and directs the MFA in Writing at Vermont College.

PETER WORTSMAN, recipient of the Beard's Fund Short Story Award, is the author of *A Modern Way to Die.* His published work includes prose poetry, essays, travelogues, interviews, and translations from the German, notably of Robert Musil and Adelbert von Chamisso.

ANDREA M. WREN's work has appeared in *Drumvoices Revue* and *Obsidian II: Black Literature in Review.* She is the associate editor of *EYEBALL,* a literary arts journal.

ROGER YEPSEN is a freelance writer and illustrator whose essays have been published in *The New York Times.* His latest book is *Apples.*

ABOUT THE PHOTOGRAPHS

Cover and title page: Rachel with great grandsons Zachery and Daniel.

Contents page: Mitsuko with her mother Masae.

Contents page: Harry and Maria with their son Anthony.

Page vii: Cathy and daughter Beth.

Page xii: The nine sisters Francis, Claudia, Jeanette, Glorida, Emma, Gwendolyn, Sylvia, Sakinah, and Debra.

Page 3: Arosylle with her sister Renu, holding baby Isa, and their mother Shyama.

Page 11: Russell with his daughter Blair.

Page 16: Family friends Nathan and Gershom.

Page 23: Ocie and her granddaughter Dora.

Page 31: Garrett and Denise watch daughter Jordan pose for the camera.

Page 37: Natalie with cousin Chelita.

Page 42: Ludmilla with her daughters Leslie and Laura, who live in neighboring towns.

Page 50: Jennifer and Mark with daughters Caroline and Kate.

Page 55: Margaret and her husband Tom.

Page 59: Rene with his aunt Yoonjeong.

Page 75: Tim with his son Rene.

Page 81: May with her mother Laura.

Page 83: First cousins Mafeesah, Sabrina, Desiree, and Fareedah.

Page 89: Fanny and her fathers Philip and Jim.

Page 94: The photographer's stepfather Bill with her niece Rebeckah.

Page 103: Efrain with his granddaughter Kayla.

Page 108: Cathy with her grandmother Rosa and sister Wendy.

Page 112: Carolyn with her grandmother Phyllis and sister Kate.

Page 116: Friends Elisabeth and Dorothy.

Page 125: Stephen with his son Arthur and his brother Mario.

Page 129: Mitsuko with parents Michael and Masae.

Page 136: Sydney, mother Ann, brother Hart, father Jerome, and sisters Eve and Colette.

Page 143: Lourdes and her son Hector.

Page 155: Tony and his band play for Gail and Horacio at their wedding

Page 161: Anu and her daughter Alina.

Page 170: Sylvia with her two sons Arthur and Michael.

Page 176: Barbara and her son Yashi.

Page 178: Shelby with her son Ray and daughter Dora.